CH

THE ART OF

BMW

MOTORCYCLES

PETER GANTRIIS

Photography by Henry von Wartenberg

motorbooks

© 2018 Quarto Publishing Group USA Inc.
Text © 2008, 2013, 2018 Peter Gantriis
Photography © 2008, 2013, 2018 Henry von Wartenberg

First published in 2008 by Motorbooks, an imprint of The Quarto Group, 401 Second Avenue North, Suite 310, Minneapolis, MN 55401 USA. This edition published in 2018.
T (612) 344-8100 F (612) 344-8692 www.QuartoKnows.com

Motorbooks titles are also available at discount for retail, wholesale, promotional, and bulk purchase. For details, contact the Special Sales Manager by email at specialsales@quarto.com or by mail at The Quarto Group, Attn: Special Sales Manager, 401 Second Avenue North, Suite 310, Minneapolis, MN 55401 USA.

10 9 8 7 6 5 4 3 2 1

ISBN: 978-0-7603-6153-5

The Library of Congress Cataloging-in-Publication Data is on file.

Acquiring Editors: Darwin Holmstorm, Kris Palmer
Art Director: Brad Springer
Project Manager: Nyle Vialet
Cover Design: Cindy Samargia Laun
Interior Design and Layout: John Barnett/4 Eyes Design, Rebecca Pagel

Printed in China

MIX
Paper from responsible sources
FSC® C104723
www.fsc.org

CONTENTS

I don't recall the exact date when I had the first contact with Peter Nettesheim. I remember a guy from the United States who sent a request to our archives to look up a few frame and engine numbers of his classic BMW motorcycles. When I did the research—we have in the BMW company archives handwritten delivery records going back to the first BMW type, the R32 from 1923—I thought, Nice collection he has! Shortly after this request, Peter announced his intent to visit the BMW headquarters in Munich. He wanted to have a look into the archives because he was seeking the history of some of his other motorcycles. I suggested that he should send us the serial numbers in advance of his visit. When he sent this list to me, I was more than impressed. I realized that this guy has one of the largest and best BMW motorcycle collections anywhere in the world.

When we had the first meeting, it started like a lot of business meetings that happened every day in a lot of countries around the world. But then I thought, This is not a meeting like usual. We went to a Munich beer garden—in Bavaria, the difference between a pub, a bar, and a restaurant is blurred—and I realized that this guy from New York is not big headed. He didn't collect the motorcycles for his self-confidence! He built up his collection because he's a real BMW enthusiast.

Since our first contact, I have met Peter Nettesheim many times, both in Germany and in the United States, where he supports a lot of events with his collection. Unforgettable, for example, is the Mastery of Speed exhibition in the American Motorcycle Association (AMA) Motorcycle Hall of Fame Museum. But he's not aloof and looks for the prime events where a lot of journalists are. With equal sincerity, he presents parts of his collection at the BMW Motorcycle Owners of America (MOA) rallies, the annual gatherings of BMW enthusiasts in North America. Over three days, he doesn't like only to show the bikes—he makes a great show. For each bike, he tells the personal story, and he starts the engine of every bike people want to hear running. And I admire him when he answers the same question for the twentieth time with the same sincerity as when he was asked for the first time.

I think a little story demonstrates Nettesheim's enthusiasm and determination. . . . In the early years, the BMW motorcycles were not produced on an assembly line. The workers built them on a special kind of table. These tables were in use at the BMW motorcycle race department through the 1950s. We have one of these tables in our historical collection, and when Peter Nettesheim heard about it, he came to Munich to take its measurements. He rebuilt two of them for special display of the early parts of his collection. For me, that shows his professionalism even more than do the perfect restorations of his motorcycles.

I'm pleased that Peter Nettesheim and his collection are the topic of a book. I wish you a pleasant story . . . and enjoy the history of BMW motorcycles.

Fred Jakobs

Fred Jakobs is responsible for BMW's motorcycle heritage collection and archives at BMW Mobile Tradition.

DAS·SCHNELLSTE·MOTORRAD·DER·WELT!
STAND VOM 1·11·1929

1923–1936

ORIGINS

The Bayerische Motorenwerke became an official entity in July of 1917. It was created as the result of a merger between two separate aircraft engine manufacturers, the Rapp Motorenwerke and the Otto-Werke. Rapp Motorenwerke had been facing some dire straits, and the merger would be a big step toward stability.

In 1913, Rapp received a large order for aircraft engines from the German armed forces. The German and Austrian forces needed the engines for their planes, as they were gearing up for conflict with the Entente Powers (Russia, France, Britain, Italy, and ultimately the United States). An arms race had broken out, and it became more intense through the first decade of the twentieth century. Rapp had been asked to produce eight- and twelve-cylinder aircraft engines to help strengthen German/Austrian air power.

In 1914, war finally broke out and threw Europe into battle. Yet when Rapp's engines proved unreliable and delivered poor performance, the military refused to order more. With a nearly dormant factory, Karl Rapp pinned his hopes on the opportunity to manufacture Austro-Daimler aerospace engines under license. Franz-Joseph Popp inspected the facility on behalf of the military and declared it suitable for the task. Popp served as production supervisor and took the company helm when Karl Rapp resigned.

The company had earned a bad reputation during the Rapp years, and military planners did not soon forget this. Seeking a fresh start, owners renamed the company Bayerische Motorenwerke GmbH in 1917 and set out to fulfill an order for Austro-Daimler licensed engines. They hired a young Max Friz to head up engineering. Friz promptly developed a new inline six-cylinder aero engine with a key technical advantage: an adjustable carburetor that could enrich the air/fuel mixture during takeoff and low-altitude operation, yet could be leaned out to accommodate the thin air at higher altitude. The new engine performed as well at higher altitudes as it did at ground level, and within only a few months, the German fighter pilots were flying planes with BMW six-cylinder power.

Through the end of the conflict, BMW continued to make aircraft engines. In 1919, pilot Franz Zeno Diemer even set a world altitude record in a BMW-powered plane, reaching more than 32,000 feet. Yet within days of Diemer's record, the warring nations signed the Treaty of Versailles, a provision that forbade Germany to manufacture military aircraft and related equipment.

If his company was to survive, Popp had to find new products to manufacture. Fortunately, engines were needed for many non-aero applications, including agriculture, truck, and marine uses, so BMW began to explore these niches to find buyers. Popp was also able to secure a contract to manufacture braking assemblies for railway cars. This large brake order put sufficient money into the coffers to keep the company alive, for the time being.

Shop foreman Martin Stolle suggested that the company explore the idea of manufacturing motorcycles. Stolle was an avid motorcyclist, and in early 1920 while the company was tooling up to manufacture railroad braking systems, he began to experiment with motorcycle engines. He developed a handful of running prototypes with their cylinders in an opposed-twin "boxer" layout dubbed the M2B15. The boxer design proved successful, and BMW received its first orders for the motorcycle engine from Victoria-Werke. Soon thereafter, BMW was able to find additional manufacturers that were interested in buying the engines, and the M2B15 was a success.

Despite the railroad air brake's profitability, Popp was eager to ditch that business. In the summer of 1922, he spun it off into a separate entity. With financial backing from wealthy Austrian Camillo Castiglioni, Popp was able to acquire the rights to the BMW name and engine designs and establish a newly independent BMW. Taking his key associates, Friz and Stolle, he moved the shop into one of Castiglioni's many factories—the site of the Bayerische Flugzeugwerke, also known as BFW.

Popp's timing was fortuitous. During World War I, BFW had made airplane components and provided maintenance and repair for the military. Like BMW, it was forced by the Versailles treaty to abandon those efforts. Led by engineer Karl Ruhmer, BFW had developed its own motorcycle—a small motorized bicycle nicknamed the "Flink." It was also building a motorcycle called the Helios, powered by BMW's M2B15 engine. It resembled an elongated bicycle with the BMW engine set longitudinally (cylinders oriented fore and aft) within the frame.

The Flink and the Helios were not popular motorcycles, however, owing mostly to their weak chassis designs. The failure of these motorcycles brought BFW to the verge of bankruptcy, yet the BMW engine had proven reliable and was praised by riders and the motoring press alike. The BMW/BFW motorcycle collaboration thus had a clear goal: develop an effective chassis to carry BMW's well-regarded engine. Popp gave the new design project to Max Friz.

Friz was reluctant at first to embark on such a project; he was an aero engineer by training, not a motorcycle designer. Yet, he did have experience with motorcycles and was willing to attack the project in his spare time while working at home.

The result of Friz's design work was the BMW R32. Friz had had experience with the Helios, and he knew that frame weakness was a critical issue for a motorcycle.

He therefore created a triangular frame, incorporating strong double-cradle spars to hold the engine and a rigid spine spanning from the steering head to the rear hub. In that engine cradle lay the M2B33 engine, an evolution of the original M2B15.

The new engine was a side-valve boxer twin that produced a modest 8.5 horsepower. It was mounted transversely across the chassis, virtually the same layout used in every BMW boxer since. This put the cylinders directly into the wind stream and solved the chronic overheating problem that plagued the rear cylinder in the Helios. This engine was also fully encased, which protected the valvetrain from road debris and in the event of a tip over. The transmission was a three-speed shifted by a hand lever mounted to the right of the fuel tank. Final drive was via a low-maintenance Cardan shaft drive—a design that was ubiquitous on bicycles of the day.

The new R32 was branded a "BMW" in an effort to set it apart from the poorly regarded BFW bikes. BMW showed the new R32 at the Paris Auto Show in the fall of 1923, and the bike caused quite a stir. While its engine wasn't especially powerful, onlookers were able to see some clever, thoughtful elements to the bike's design. It was also clear that the R32 was created with two key criteria in mind: ease of maintenance and reliability.

It's difficult to overstate how important these attributes were in the eyes of 1920s motorcycle owners. Motorcycles were viewed as essential transportation tools—they were inexpensive to buy, simple to operate, and capable of traveling to just about anywhere. Most owners performed the simple mainte-nance tasks themselves, and no one wants to be stranded by a mechanical failure while riding. The BMW R32 addressed these con-cerns. Its Cardan shaft drive required far less maintenance than belt or chain drives. Valve adjustments were performed relatively eas-ily, since the transverse orientation of the engine provided easy access to the cylinder

heads. Features like these, in combination with BMW's growing reputation for quality and reliability, made the R32 a noteworthy bike and helped justify its premium price.

The R32 went into production in late 1923, and it formed the basis for BMW's motorcycle designs through the prewar period. More than 3,000 R32 bikes were produced between 1923 and 1926. BMW steadily refined the R32 and successive models, addressing concerns and failures and improving the motorcycles' overall performance. In addition, BMW raced and rallied its bikes to build brand awareness and test its motorcycles' technology.

BMW's rivals included Victoria, which had hired Martin Stolle as its chief engineer. BMW's early efforts to compete with Victoria proved unsuccessful, and the company suf-fered embarrassing defeat in the Stuttgart races of 1923. Yet BMW was pushing new technology into its racing efforts. Young BMW engineer Rudolf Schleicher had devel-oped a new boxer engine variant featuring an overhead-cam cylinder head. The engine, called the M2B36, would help BMW claim racing victories in the ensuing years. Key among these victories was Schleicher's win at the prestigious six-day race in England in 1926. Schleicher claimed victory on an R37, and the international press heralded BMW's competitive success. To make Schleicher's feat even more impressive, he had accom-plished it not on a specially prepped race bike, but on a true series-produced motor-cycle shod with conventional road tires!

Success in the racing program gave BMW the confidence to continue developing new motorcycles and pushing new technologies. In 1927, BMW launched the R47, and in 1928, the company launched four new models. BMW's strategy was to use a common chassis to build both sporting and touring models to broaden the product portfolio. The sporting models typically featured higher-horsepower overhead-cam engines. Like today's sportbikes,

these models were targeted at the buyer who wanted a spirited motorcycle for personal use—a machine that had much in common with the factory's racing bikes. The touring models were more utilitarian and were powered by torquey side-valve boxer engines. Sidecar rigs were essential vehicles in the prewar era; they were used for tasks like mail and package delivery, law enforcement, and military transportation. BMW's touring models typically featured a sidecar and were built with reliability and serviceability as their key strengths.

While the boxers represented BMW's top of the line, the company also manufactured economical single-cylinder bikes during the 1920s. The R39 was introduced in 1925, but was discontinued in 1927 due to slow sales. Production of single-cylinder bikes resumed in 1931 with the 200-cc R2, followed by the 400-cc R4.

The motorcycle business was growing nicely for BMW in the late 1920s. In 1926, the company also was able to resume manufacturing aero engines and, in 1928, ventured into automobile production. BMW purchased the Eisenach factory and began to build a line of tiny autos under license from Britain's Austin. Motorcycle racing efforts also continued steadily through the '20s and into the '30s, with star rider Ernest Henne setting many world motorcycle speed records on his BMWs throughout this period.

The "pressed steel" models defined BMW's bikes of the 1930s. These chassis were stronger than the tubular steel predeces-sors, though many enthusiasts find the earlier bikes more elegant. Nevertheless, the motorcycles needed stronger frames, and the welding and metallurgy of the day did not allow BMW to continue using tubular frames. Of course, in the late 1930s, geopolitical developments were overshadowing the world of motorcycling, and reliable vehicle and engine manufacturer, BMW, would again be pulled into war production.

1925 R32

First shown at the Paris Salon of 1923, the R32 represented the state of the art of motorcycle design in the early 1930s. Its triangular frame and compact driveline gave it a distinctively tight, low profile, and the technological developments in the bike would shape BMW's designs for decades to come.

The heart of the R32 was its new engine. Labeled the M2B33, the R32's engine was built with reliability and ease of maintenance as the primary design criteria. This new engine displaced 494 cc, with 68-millimeter bore and stroke measurements. It was a wet-sump design, with oil pumps that circulated the oil. This was a significant technological advancement and, unlike the total-loss oiling systems of the day, it did not require the owner to add oil at regular intervals.

Where the preceding engine design (the M2B15) was intended for a fore-and-aft cylinder arrangement, the new engine was mounted transversely across the frame. This had several key benefits. First and foremost, the cylinders were now protruding into the airflow around the bike, which dramatically improved the cylinder cooling and servicing. The side-valve cylinder head made valve adjustments very easy to perform. Finally, this drivetrain layout made it practical to connect the transmission directly to the engine case, eliminating the need for a primary drive system that might require periodic maintenance.

The R32's chassis situated the engine low, keeping the center of gravity low and making the bike easier to handle. The new engine/transmission layout also made practical a shaft final drive. Shaft drive requires much less maintenance than a belt or chain and has the added benefit of facilitating wheel and tire changes. The importance of this feature cannot be overstated, as many R32s traveled rough roads, and their tires were frequently punctured. Speaking of rough roads, the R32 offered a leaf-spring front suspension for the front wheel and a sprung seat compensated for the rigid rear suspension.

By today's standards, the R32's performance was not exceptional. The M2B33 engine produced a modest 8.5 horsepower and propelled the motorcycle to a top speed of about 60 miles per hour. But in its day, this was adequate performance for a motorcycle, considering that most riders would cruise at speeds in the 40-mile-per-hour range. Significantly, the R32 also had excellent fuel economy. It could travel more than 80 miles on a gallon of fuel, making it a very practical machine for daily use. The 3.7-gallon fuel tank gave the bike a comfortable range for touring.

| THE ART OF BMW

THE ART OF BMW

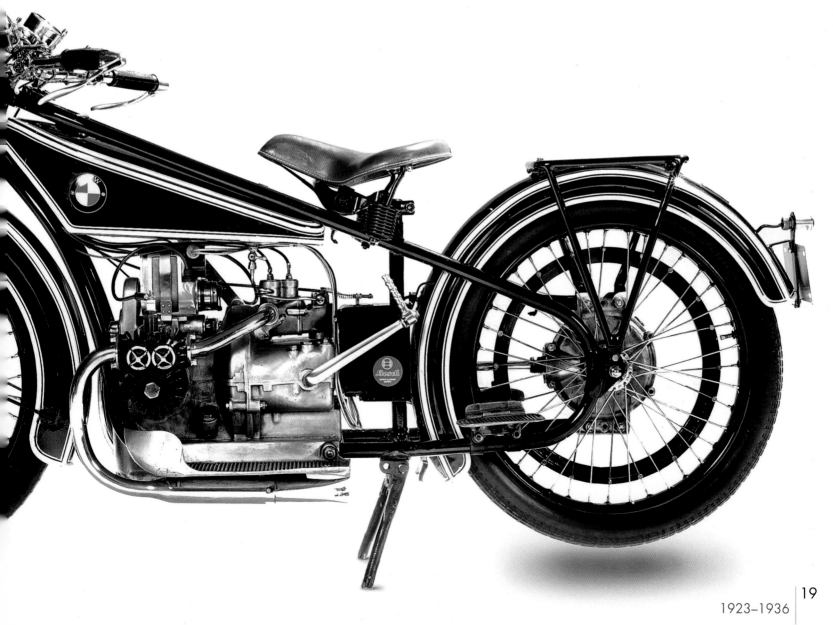

1927 R47

In 1926, the R32 was joined by a sibling, the R37. The R37 shared a chassis with the R32, but it was considered an aggressive, sporting motorcycle and was powered by an overhead-valve (OHV) engine (versus the R32's side-valve arrangement). The OHV M2B36 engine offered a nice increase in performance; it could produce 16 horsepower, compared with the R32's 8.5. The improved airflow to the cylinder heads enabled the engine to run a higher compression ratio and at a higher rpm range.

Lubrication of an OHV cylinder head proved to be a challenge, but in typical fashion BMW's engineers developed some unique solutions. Early BMW OHV engines incorporated three separate oil sumps. The first was located in the main engine case and operated by a high pressure oil pump, which lubricated the crank, cam, lifters, and gear train. The roller bearing rocker arms were lubricated by their own separate oil sump in each cylinder head.

Once the valve cover was installed, they were filled with 250 milliliters of oil, and the valves were now able to get adequate splash to lubricate the bearings in the cylinder heads.

By the end of 1926, the R42 replaced the R32. The R42 was powered by an updated side-valve engine that produced 12 horsepower. This engine, the M43a, retained the "square" 68-millimeter bore and stroke measurements, but new alloy cylinder heads and an improved carburetor increased performance. The R42 retained a three-speed transmission, while engineers improved the model's braking abilities with an expanding-shoe front brake and a rear brake that applied its braking force to the driveshaft. A new frame cradled the engine in a lower position and further back, thus creating a lower center of gravity. With these engine and chassis improvements, the R42 proved much more capable than the R32, especially when mounted with a sidecar.

The R47 was introduced in 1927, and it succeeded the R37 as the performance model in the BMW lineup. At a price of DM 1,850, the R47 was considerably more expensive than an R42 (DM 1,510), but priced far below the outgoing R37 (DM 2,900). The R47 shared the same chassis as the R42, but its engine produced 18 horsepower and could propel the R47 to a top speed of 68 miles per hour.

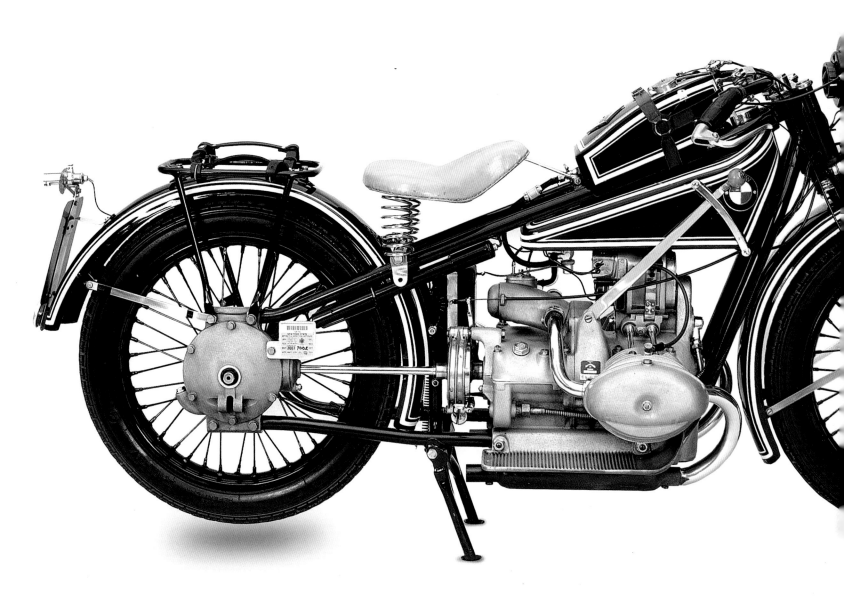

1927 Bayerische **R47**
Motoren
Werke AG München

1928 R52

By 1928, BMW was preparing to make some significant changes to its engine lineup. Racing had taught the company some valuable lessons, and the motorcycle market was rewarding BMW's performance and technology advancements. BMW sales were growing nicely, and the company recognized that there was room in the marketplace for more than two BMW models at a time.

The R52 was introduced as a replacement for the R42. The R52 would fill the role of touring motorcycle, priced at an attainable DM 1,510 (the same price as the R42). The R52 was powered by a new version of the side-valve boxer, marked the M57. Though displacement was nearly the same as the M43a engine, the 486-cc M57 did not retain the "square" bore and stroke measurements of the M43a. Instead, the engine received a 63-millimeter bore and 78-millimeter stroke.

These internals were installed in an engine case that had some rather unique features. The rear was completely enclosed—an engineering strategy that substantially increased the engine case's strength in the area around the rear bearing retainer, which was under a great deal of stress. The downside of this strategy was that clutch service was quite difficult. However, the BMW engineers were facing some serious issues with weak castings. Metallurgy of the late 1920s was nowhere near as advanced as it is today, and BMW engineers needed to form the back of the case in this manner to add strength. As casting processes and metal quality improved, this very non-service-friendly casting was no longer necessary.

The new internals mildly altered the engine's power and torque curves, but the R52's performance was nearly identical to that of the outgoing R42, and peak horsepower output was virtually identical. The R52 could attain a top speed of 62 miles per hour, and it achieved a still excellent fuel economy of 67 miles per gallon. Best of all, the long-stroke engine generated a bit more mid-range torque and was better suited for sidecar duties.

This updated side-valve engine was mounted in a new frame, designated the F56. This frame was to be shared across three additional models from the period: the R57, the R62, and R63. BMW produced almost 4,400 R52s.

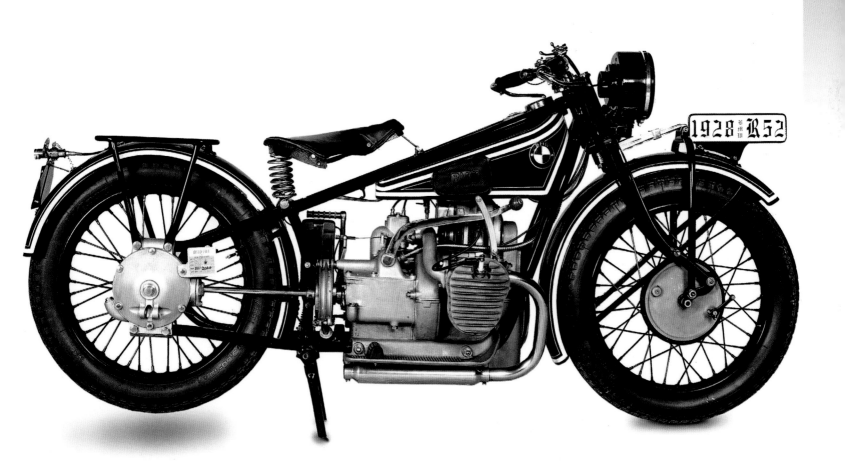

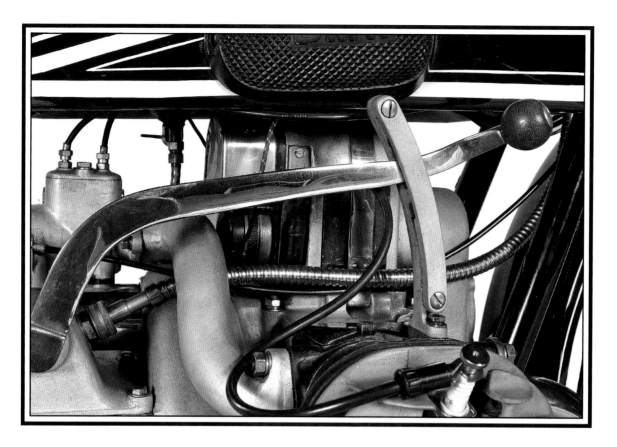

THE ART OF BMW

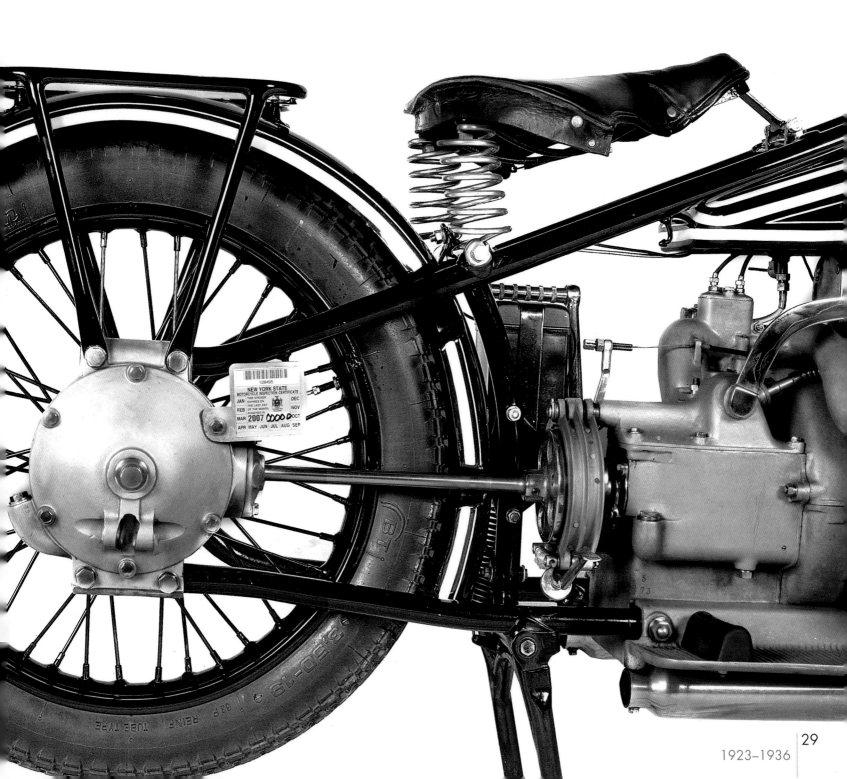

1928 R57

The R57 had much in common with the R47 it replaced. Its engine featured the familiar "square" bore and stroke at 68 millimeters and matched its predecessor's 18 horsepower output. However, there were some key evolutionary changes that affected the R57's performance. Key among them was an improved transmission and electrical system. This series of incremental improvements was not unlike the current evolution of the modern sportbike.

In 1928, Bosch improved the BMW boxers' magneto ignition system with higher voltage and an optional generator to better power lights. The value of a strong ignition system cannot be overstated, considering the variable quality of fuel and state of tuning during the 1920s. Contrary to today's riders, motorcyclists then were not required to have lighting nor did they necessarily desire it. BMW's sporting motorcycles were typically devoid of headlights or taillights,

emphasizing the no-frills aggressive nature of the sport-oriented machines, but by 1929, lighting was standard equipment on all BMWs.

To meet sidecar owners' needs, BMW's engineers gave the R57 a clutch update that incorporated two plates, rather than one in the dry clutch. Like all BMWs, the R57 was also available with an optional, shorter final drive ratio.

Considering its sporting intent, the R57's chassis and suspension received some minor improvements to enhance the bike's handling. The wheelbase was shortened by 10 millimeters, and the fuel capacity was reduced due to a revised fuel tank shape. The front brake was enlarged to 200 millimeters, providing improved stopping power and compensating for the weak brake shoe at the rear wheel. Unfortunately, the R57's curb weight grew by 45 pounds, which likely negated any performance gains to be had from the driveline and chassis refinements.

BMW produced about 1,000 R57 motorcycles, which was substantially less than the 1,700 R47 bikes to leave the factory. This was likely due to two factors: a 20 percent price premium over the outgoing R47 model, and competition from the stout 750-cc side-valve R62, available for DM 1,650.

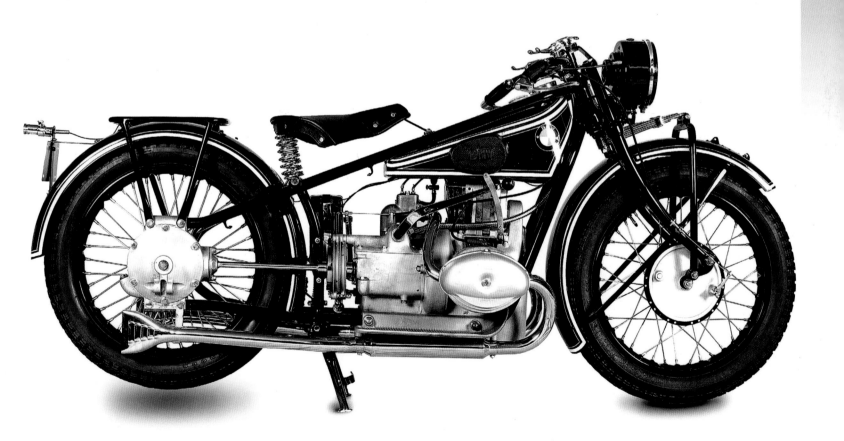

1929 R62

The R62 and its stablemate, the R63, added dimension to the BMW lineup. The R62 shared the same frame as the R52, R57, and R63, but it was powered by a larger-displacement version of the side-valve boxer. The 745-cc R62 generated 18 horsepower and significantly more torque than the 486-cc side-valve R52. Priced a mere 10 percent more than an R52, the R62 attracted customers in equal numbers. BMW produced 4,300 of the R62 models.

This new 745-cc engine was closely related to its smaller-displacement side-valve sibling in the R52. It had "square" bore and stroke measurements (78 millimeters), and a compression ratio of 5.5:1. The engine was mated to a three-speed transmission, which was available with sidecar final drive gearing (1:5.18 final drive ratio); the engine retained BMW's unique flywheel air intake system.

Flywheel intake? Well, at the time when the R62 was built, air filtration was in a primitive state. BMW engineers didn't have access to sophisticated filters, much less today's nanofilter technology. But naturally, motorcycle engines needed to breathe fresh air in some rugged conditions. BMW's engineers needed to design an intake system that could supply dry, clean air, and they developed some clever solutions to the problem.

Since air filters were not commonly applied to motorcycle engines, the engineers' first goal was to increase the length of the engine's intake tract. This allowed more surface area for particles in the intake air to collect on before they could be pulled into the combustion chamber. Next, BMW's engineers selected an unusual location for air to enter the engine. These air inlets were located on the side of the engine case, behind each horizontal cylinder. This air inlet location has several key benefits: First, the air intake is protected from debris and water splash by the protruding cylinders themselves. Second, the intake air is preheated by the hot cylinder, shortening the engine's warm-up time. Finally, as the air circumvents the engine's spinning flywheel, the latter acts as a centrifugal cleaner before the air enters the intake runners. Once filtered, the intake air then doubles back through the carburetor and down the long intake tubes. This clever intake system was a unique feature that helped ensure that BMW engines breathed fresh air without the aid of an air filter.

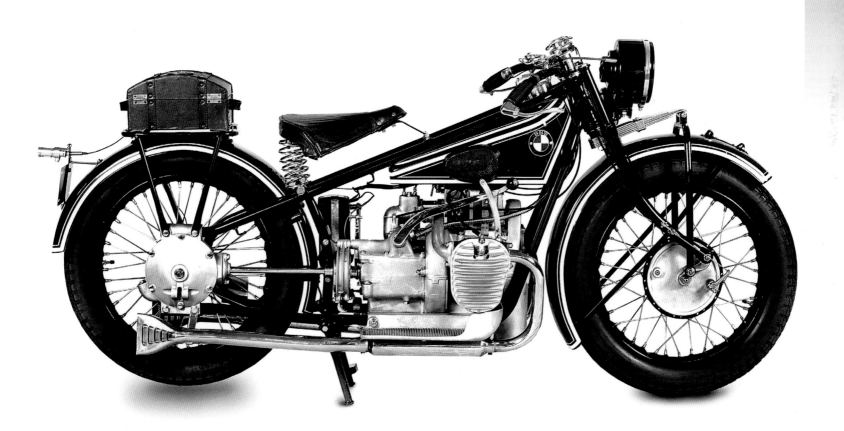

1928 R63

Introduced in 1928, the R63 was BMW's "superbike." Built on the F56 chassis, the R63 was true to the fledgling company's competitive spirit. BMW had been racing 750-cc motorcycles for two years before offering the high-performance R63, and the racing development helped shape the street-going bike's new 735-cc OHV powerplant.

This new OHV engine, designated the M60, had a power band very different from its side-valve stablemate. This was a high-revving engine with an 83-millimeter bore and a short 68-millimeter stroke, and alloy pistons replacing the previous cast-iron slugs. The M60 was rated at 24 horsepower at 4,000 rpm, though performance suggested this was a conservative output rating. In stock form, the R63 could attain a top speed of 74 miles per hour, making it one of the fastest motorcycles on the market. It was also one of the most expensive motorcycles, priced at DM 2,100.

Naturally, such a powerful superbike would find its way to the track; racing and record-setting were very important to BMW in the 1920s. Racing success established BMW's reputation for building fine sporting motorcycles. It also directly influenced the company's production motorcycles, revealing weaknesses and creating opportunities to experiment with new engine and chassis technologies. The knowledge BMW gained from extreme competition led to a unique pair of new models.

1931 R16

From the late 1920s until World War II, BMW motorcycles were competitive in both road-racing and top-speed racing events. Winners of these competitions were highly regarded, and for good reason; it took a special type of rider to pilot a supercharged hardtail motorcycle at speeds of over 130 miles per hour. BMW had its hero in Ernst Henne, whose efforts gave BMW its first of many speed records on a supercharged 750. In September 1929, Henne pushed a BMW 750 to a world motorcycle speed record of 134.78 miles per hour on a closed course near Munich. More records followed as Henne and BMW competed with other manufacturers like Gilera and Brough Superior.

As a direct result of its racing development work, BMW was able to address weaknesses in the tube-steel frames that formed the backbone of bikes like the R63. These tube-steel frames were prone to breaking, particularly when subjected to the stresses of supporting a sidecar. There were also instances of collapsing front forks, as the bikes were pounded over Europe's ancient roads. BMW crafted a solution to these problems, called the R16.

Introduced in 1929, the R16 was built on an all-new pressed-steel frame. This frame had much in common with its predecessors, including a familiar twin-loop design and a virtually identical plate-spring trailing-link front suspension setup. However, the new frame added some much-needed torsional rigidity, making it better able to withstand the rigors of sidecar duty and high-performance riding. The downside of this added strength was a 22-pound weight increase.

The R16 was propelled by the same OHV engine that powered the R63. This M60 engine received some upgrades, though, to improve its power output. In 1932, BMW replaced the three-jet BMW carb with twin Amal carburetors. The upgrades yielded significant gains, bringing output of the 736-cc engine to 33 horsepower at 4,500 rpm. Top speed was also increased to 78 miles per hour.

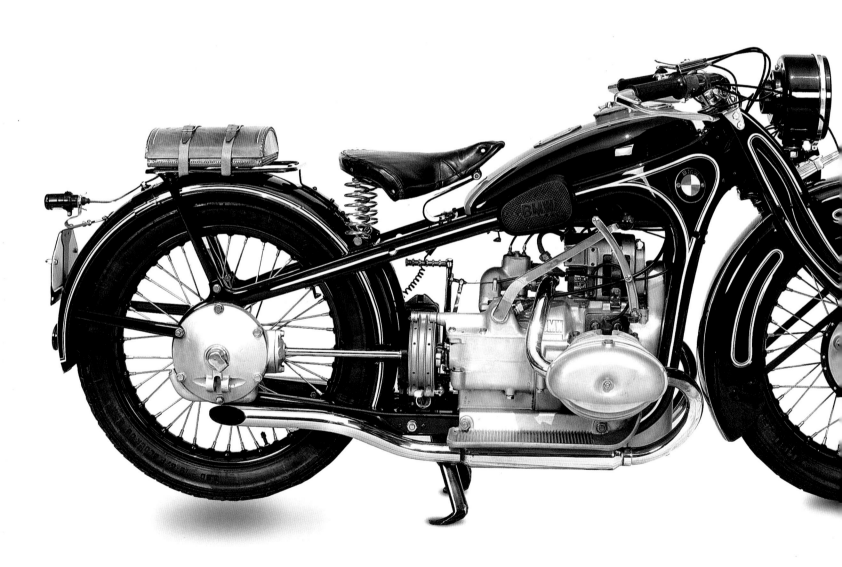

1934 R11

The R11 was a sibling to the R16. Also introduced in 1929, the R11 replaced the R62 as BMW's touring motorcycle. Built around the same pressed-steel frame as the R16, the R11 used the outgoing R62's side-valve engine. By 1934 the R11's 745-cc side-valve M56 engine was tuned to produce 20 horsepower.

Between 1929 and 1934, BMW offered five versions, or "series", of both the R11 and R16. The company continually refined its bikes through this period, making incremental improvements to the chassis, brakes, engine, and controls. The five series of the R11 and R16 set a naming convention that BMW would carry through the 1960s.

The Series 2 R11 and R16 bikes were released in 1930. At that time, both bikes received larger-diameter Cardan brakes to improve stopping power at the rear wheel. More significant changes appeared with the Series 3 bikes in 1932. The R11 Series 3 received a new Sum carburetor that provided preheated, secondary air-injection from the exhaust manifold. The R16 Series 3 featured twin carburetors and its compression ratio increased to 7:1, which pushed output to 33 brake horsepower.

Incremental improvements continued through 1934, with the Series 4 and Series 5 models. For 1933, the only change for the Series 4 R11 was a revised shift lever, mounted on the right side of the tank. However, for the 1934 Series 5 model, BMW added a dual-carburetor setup to the side-valve engine. Drawing fuel through twin Amal carbs, the R11 could now produce 20 horsepower and attain a top speed of 69 miles per hour. Even though the twin carbs offered significant performance advantages, some single-carb versions of the bike were produced for the military. In total, approximately 7,500 R11 bikes were produced during the 1929–1934 period, outselling the R16 at a ratio of more than seven to one.

1936 R5

Deriving much of its new design from BMW's racing efforts, the R5 was a sensation when introduced in 1936. The R5 featured a new chassis, a new engine, and major suspension and control improvements. By today's standards, the R5 would be characterized as a "bargain sport-bike," as it rolled all of these advanced new features into a stylish package offered at a very competitive price.

The basis of this new bike was a well-designed new frame that drew heavily from BMW's racing development experiences. Metallurgy and assembly techniques were improving rapidly at BMW, allowing the engineers to use tubular steel for the new R5 frame. Unlike previous tube-frame bikes like the R63, the R5's new frame had tubes with an oval-shaped cross-section. Improved electrical welding made the joints much stronger, and the new frame achieved remarkable rigidity. Best of all, the R5's frame was not nearly as heavy as the pressed-steel frames of the R11 or R16, enabling the new R5 to tip the scales at an excellent 363 pounds.

In addition to the lightweight frame, the R5 received a sweet powerplant—a potent and race-proven 494-cc OHV boxer. The all-new engine featured a revised valvetrain, incorporating two camshafts driven by a timing chain. The engine case was no longer a split-housing, but a single casting. New cylinder head assemblies included rocker arm bearings that were cast into the heads and valve springs that were better suited to high-rpm operation. The result was a powerplant that produced 24 horsepower at 5,500 rpm—almost the same output as the OHV engine in the early R16 models.

To deliver the power, the R5 was fitted with a four-speed transmission. A key feature of this transmission was the new shifter location by the rider's left foot. The R5 also had a vestigial shift lever on the right side of the case, ostensibly to enable inexperienced riders to find neutral easily. However, it is likely that this hand-shift lever was rarely used once the rider became accustomed to the left-foot shifting action.

Of particular note on the R5 is its front suspension. The new motorcycle featured a telescopic fork that even allowed for external damping adjustment. This setup is ubiquitous in today's motorcycling world, but telescopic forks were a breakthrough in the 1930s. Although front-wheel travel was limited and the bike retained a rigid rear suspension setup, this new front suspension still offered superior wheel control and contributed significantly to the bike's handling and sporting character.

Overall, the R5 represented an excellent value for money. Priced at DM 1,550, it cost DM 500 less than the R17 and was even priced below the R12. For that price, a buyer was getting a very capable 500-cc sporting motorcycle that was built around some of the best technology available. Its performance was a match for 750-cc motorcycles, and its nimble handling made it a delight to ride.

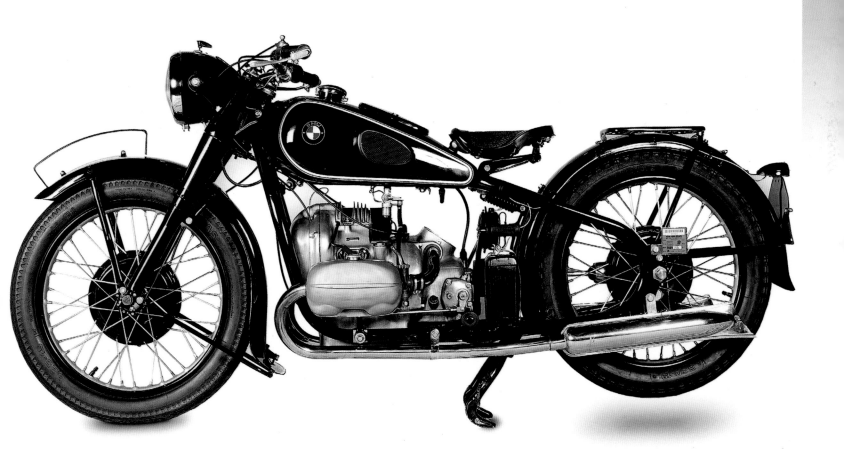

1937–1969

BMW continued to build its inexpensive single-cylinder bikes throughout the 1930s. The 200-cc R2 was a popular model, since the rider was not required to have a motorcycle license to operate a bike up to 200 cc. The single-cylinder range was also expanded to help "bridge the gap" between the singles and the larger-displacement boxer-powered models. These models included the 300-cc R3 and the 400-cc R4. The R3 was a failure, since it had neither the R4's power nor the R2's licensing exemption. But the R4 found many buyers. It was not a spectacular performer, but it was very affordable transportation at a time when autos were still prohibitively expensive. The R4 was also popular as a fleet vehicle, and it was purchased in large numbers by the military and local police forces. BMW would later build the R35, a single that descended from the R4, but featured the new telescopic front fork.

WORLD WAR II

Production of civilian motorcycles came to a halt in 1940. Germany was by now fully engaged in conflict, and the nation's industrial power was redirected to support the military effort. BMW had been selling motorcycles to the military for years, and there were already many R2, R4, and R35 models, along with R12 sidecar haulers, in the military fleet.

But the military's needs were evolving, and BMW (along with its rival, Zundapp) was asked to produce a sidecar motorcycle that would be more effective for the armed forces. Particularly, the military needed a bike that was reliable and robust enough to survive extended periods at low marching speeds—where the engine was below its power band and cooling air across the cylinders was

minimal. The bikes had to be powerful enough to move three fully burdened soldiers, plus a bit of additional armament and gear. The military also demanded that the bike be capable of off-road travel over rough terrain. Of course, all of this was required without having to sacrifice reliability. So in 1938 BMW began developing what would become the R75. BMW would ultimately manufacture this motorcycle at the Eisenach facility and, from 1941 to 1944, would produce approximately 18,000 examples for the German military.

Allied bombings battered BMW's facilities, making mass production a challenging proposition. The Eisenach factory, which was making both autos and motorcycles, was a frequent target. The Munich facility was making aero engines for the German military, so it too was a primary bombing objective. Air raid destruction reduced the facilities' output. By the end of the war, virtually every building that BMW had been using was damaged by the bombings.

POSTWAR

The entire company was in shambles after the war. Not only were the physical structures severely damaged, but also most of the motorcycle blueprints had been lost during the conflict. The Eisenach facility was located in what would become East Germany.

There were some glimmers of hope when the conflict ended, though. The American occupiers needed a facility where they could repair and maintain their vehicle fleets. They used BMW's Munich facility and employed its staff with maintenance tasks. The facility was also used to manufacture household items and even some bicycles.

The staff wanted to resume manufacturing motor vehicles, however. BMW was granted permission to produce motorcycles on the condition that its engines displaced less than 250 cc. Since the company's plans and blueprints were lost, engineers tore down some surviving motorcycles and measured each component as accurately as possible. They used this information as the basis of the plans for a new motorcycle, the R24.

BMW showed the public the R24 in the spring of 1948 and began manufacturing the bikes as quickly as possible. Unfortunately, material shortages delayed the delivery of the bikes for about six months; dealers did not begin to receive the motorcycles until December. There was a great deal of pent-up demand for the bikes. Germans needed affordable transportation, and the BMW fit the bill nicely. Despite a number of competitors that offered less expensive, smaller-displacement two-stroke bikes, BMW's motorcycles were in high demand. The BMW reputation for quality and racing success in the prewar years had been successfully carried forward to the postwar marketplace. Buyers were clamoring for the bikes, and even the German president's security detail rode the single-cylinder "Beemers." The R24 would ultimately be supplanted in 1950 by the R25, a more refined model that offered rear suspension. BMW would build many R25s for a hungry postwar marketplace; its production topped 23,000 units in its first year alone.

In 1950, occupying forces permitted BMW to resume production of its larger-displacement boxer-powered bikes. BMW took up the opportunity by launching the R51/2, a mildly updated version of the prewar R51. This bike was also a success; the public bought more than 5,000 units in the first year. The company continued developing the R51 through the first part of the decade, adding a new model, the R68.

The sporting R68 was a postwar breakthrough for BMW. The bike's performance was stellar for the day, its 35 horsepower engine propelling it to a 100-mile-per-hour top speed. Serious sporting motorcyclists snapped up the bike despite its premium price of DM 4,000.

BMW's motorcycle production levels grew steadily through the 1950s, peaking at about 30,000 bikes in 1955. By the mid-1950s, though, the automobile was beginning to put the brakes on motorcycle sales growth. As the German economy rebounded from the war, buyers aspired to own an automobile, and BMW's moto sales began to suffer. In 1952, the company restarted its auto manufacturing and was producing the very unique Isetta subcompact car. Growth in the auto business was quickly on track to outpace the motorcycle business, and much of BMW's resources became focused on automobile products.

Nevertheless, BMW bikes were receiving new features and technology. By the mid-1950s, the company had made major chassis updates, including the Earles fork front suspension. Racing efforts were integral to the development of new technologies, and Georg "Schorsch" Meier and Walter Zeller were bringing much attention to the high-performing BMW bikes in the German racing championships. However, by 1957, BMW's motorcycle successes had reached a zenith, and the company's fortunes would take a downward turn at the end of the decade.

By 1960, BMW was staggering under the weight of its ailing auto business. Its six-cylinder models had not been well received, and debts were mounting. At its darkest hour in December 1959, a buyout offer from Daimler-Benz was rebuffed, and with the help of banker Herbert Quandt, BMW was able to avert a complete collapse. Quandt's capital infusion helped to spark the company's product-development efforts, but the effects were felt more quickly in the automotive division, and they took some years to reach the motorcycle group.

The automotive side of BMW's portfolio grew rapidly through the 1960s. By 1969, motorcycles represented only 5 percent of BMW's sales revenue; it was utterly dwarfed by the rebounding automotive sales. As a result, the motorcycle division became a bit of a corporate backwater. BMW made only nominal product updates to its bikes during the early '60s.

Motorcycle staff began to see glimmers of hope in 1967. That year BMW offered three key new models for export: the R50 US, R60 US, and R69S. The renewed development efforts these bikes reflected were important for the company, as competition from other motorcycle manufacturers had increased. Automobile production continued to dominate the BMW landscape, so much so that by 1969 the company was forced to relocate its motorcycle production to Berlin to make way for expanded auto production at the Munich plant. Having its own factory proved beneficial for the motorcycle division, however. Changes were afoot, and the bikes from the Berlin factory would be pivotal in a BMW motorcycle renaissance.

1937 R12

1941 R12

Business was booming at BMW in the mid-1930s. Total production increased dramatically in 1934 to almost 10,000 motorcycles, and the company was maintaining its momentum with continuous product development.

While not nearly as attractive-looking as their predecessors, the R11 and R16 pressed-steel models proved to be workhorse motorcycles, and they sold in significant numbers. Their stout frames made them ideal for sidecar applications and also helped the bikes endure the roughest road conditions, making them indispensable to the German armed forces. In early 1935, BMW unveiled updated versions of the pressed-steel bikes. Dubbed the R12 and R17, these bikes carried on with the robust pressed-steel frame, yet they integrated some new drivetrain and chassis technology.

Powered by the same basic 745-cc engine as the R11, the R12 featured either a single carburetor or a dual-carb setup. The single-carb engine produced the same 18 horsepower as it did in the R11, while its dual carb sibling produced 20 horses. The single-carb version was the choice of Germany's armed forces, which likely valued the simplicity of a single-carb engine for ease of maintenance and reliability. These engines were mated to a new four-speed transmission.

The real significance of the R12 lay in its updated chassis. When introduced in 1935, the R12 and its sibling, the R17, were the first motorcycles in the world to be fitted with a hydraulic telescopic front fork. Though it had a limited range of travel, the fork vastly improved ride quality and was very similar in design to the front forks of most of today's motorcycles. Despite the breakthrough technology of this front suspension, the R12 and R17 were still built with a rigid rear suspension; shock absorbers and springs would not appear on a BMW motorcycle until 1937.

Rounding out the changes to the R12 was a new rear braking system with a 200-millimeter drum. This was a great improvement over the previous Cardan brake, which applied its braking force to the driveshaft. The new rear drum was the same size as the drum on the front wheel, and the front and rear wheels were interchangeable. The wheels also used the ubiquitous 3.5x19 tires that other manufacturers used, making it easier to find replacement tires.

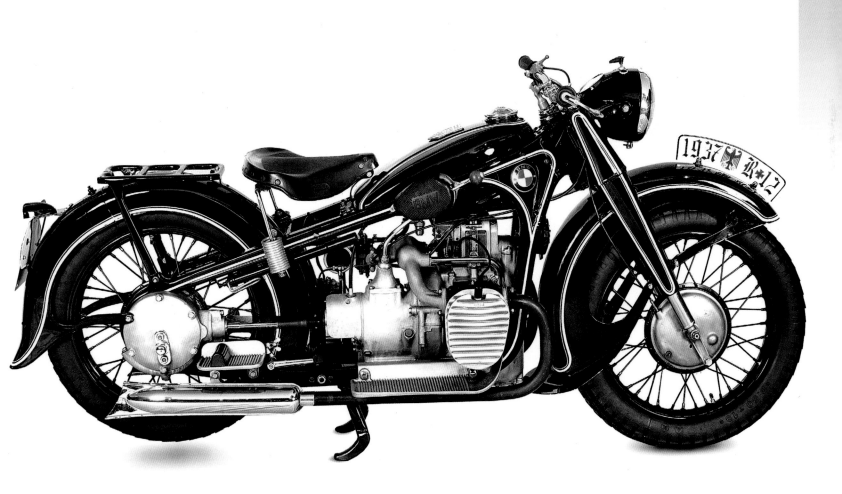

THE ART OF BMW

1937 R35

While BMW focused much of its development efforts on the larger-displacement boxer twins, it maintained a solid presence in the single-cylinder market throughout the '30s. The singles served as mainstream bikes aimed at the rider who wanted economical transportation and bulletproof reliability, yet they were closely related to their larger-displacement, boxer-powered cousins. Technology and design changes initiated on the larger bikes trickled down to the singles in the form of engine components, chassis refinements, and better suspension and controls—all offered at an attractive price. The R35 is a prime example of this strategy.

The R35 was the last BMW single to utilize a pressed-steel frame, even as other models in the BMW lineup used the new, improved tubular frames. The R35 also used a simpler version of the telescoping front fork, which did not utilize

hydraulic damping. Both of these product decisions saved manufacturing costs for this budget-minded model.

Despite its humble basic components, the bike would prove to be a solid performer and a showroom success. The R35 was propelled by an OHV 342-cc single-cylinder engine that produced 14 horsepower at 3,500 rpm. This vertical single-cylinder engine was matched to a four-speed transmission controlled via a hand-shift on the right side of the bike. This powertrain could bring the R35 to a top speed of 62 miles per hour, yet sip fuel at the rate of 78 miles per gallon.

The R35's simplicity and economy made it very attractive to the military. Its 342-cc engine was proven, and the pressed-steel frame was a positive attribute for military use, where strength and function were more important than aesthetic appeal. As a result, the German military bought the R35 in large numbers for use primarily as courier bikes.

The R35 was built at BMW's Eisenach plant, which was located in what was to become East Germany after the war. Later versions remained in production until 1955, long after the end of World War II, and the bike's total production exceeded 80,000 units. Later models received some significant chassis upgrades, notably the "plunger" rear suspension, which would improve the ride quality somewhat.

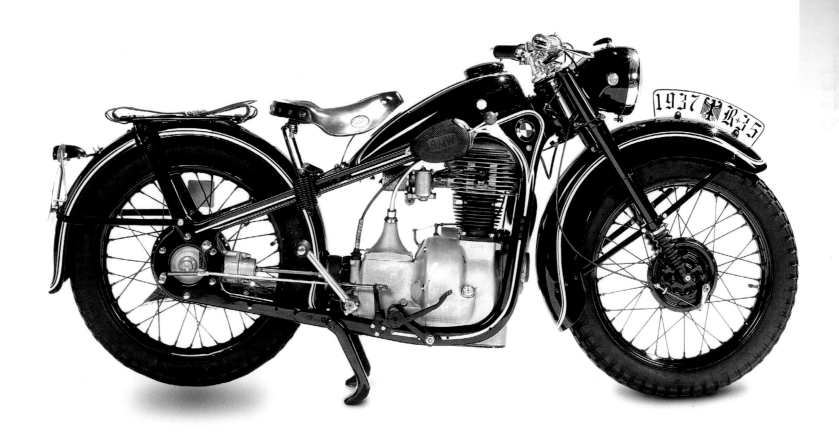

THE ART OF BMW

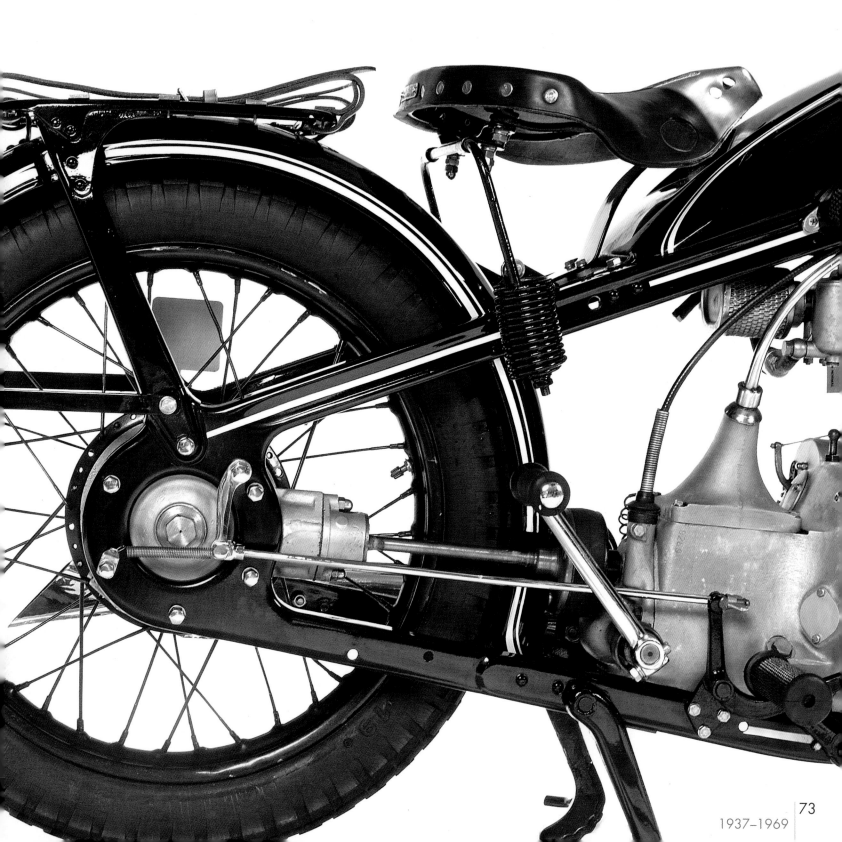

1941 R71

In 1938, BMW brought out four new boxer-powered models, all based on a new tubular-steel, dual-cradle, fully sprung chassis. With this new chassis, dubbed the 251/1, BMW engineers finally integrated a rear suspension setup, a design that was tested on the racetrack in 1937. The layout that BMW engineers chose was a plunger-type telescopic rear suspension. The design incorporated a large shock absorber on each side of the rear wheel, and the shocks allowed approximately 2 inches of vertical suspension travel. The driveshaft was also fitted with a universal joint to allow it ample flexibility when the suspension compressed. The front of the bike retained the familiar telescopic fork.

Two of BMW's new motorcycles were built to supersede existing BMW models. The new R51 took the place of the R5, retaining the 494-cc OHV powerplant. The R61 supplanted the R6, carrying over its 600-cc side-valve mill. But there were also two all-new models that expanded the BMW lineup: the R66 and the R71.

The new OHV R66 was positioned as BMW's top-of-the-line sporting motorcycle. Its 597-cc OHV engine was fueled by twin Amal carburetors and matched to a four-speed transmission. This engine produced 30 horsepower at 5,300 rpm and could push the R66 to a top speed of 90 miles per hour.

The final new model was the R71. Designed primarily as a sidecar motorcycle, the R71 was designated to replace the aging R12. Its power came from the familiar side-valve 746-cc engine fed by twin Graetzin carburetors. This engine made 22 horsepower and plenty of torque for sidecar use, but it would prove to be the last side-valve that BMW ever produced.

The 1941 R71 in these photographs is among a small number of bikes produced for civilian use during World War II. Germany was, of course, fully engaged in conflict during that year, and BMW would soon be required to devote its manufacturing effort to producing war-related materiel. Nevertheless, the company produced a final run of civilian R71 motorcycles in the spring of 1941. In May of that year, BMW discontinued all civilian motorcycles. The government required it to manufacture only aircraft engines and its military-spec R75 motorcycles, which were also introduced in 1941.

THE ART OF BMW

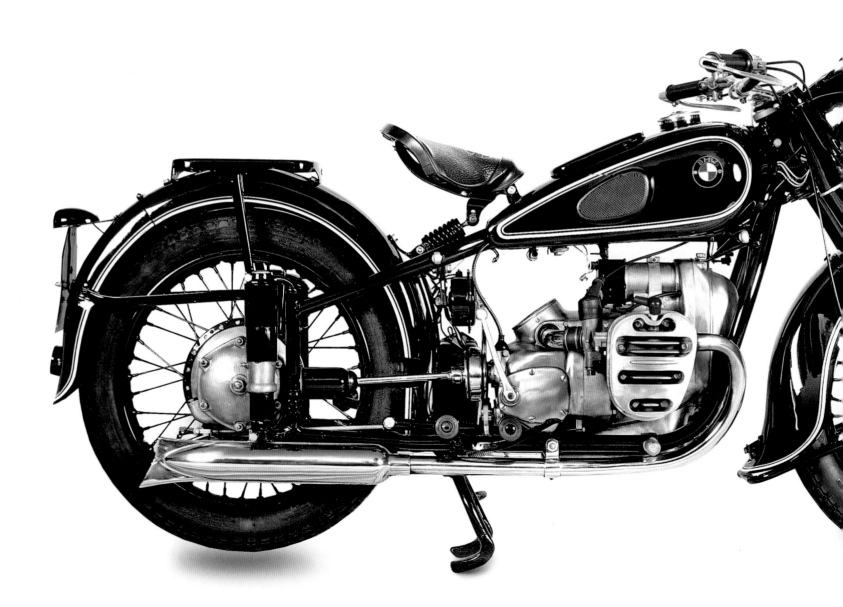

THE ART OF BMW

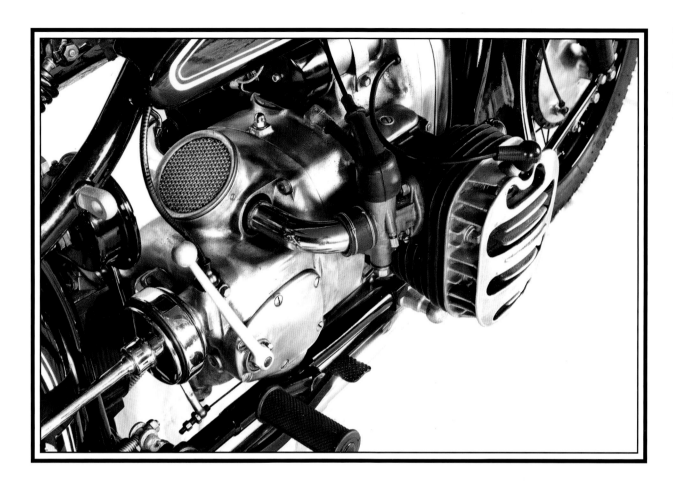

1942 R75M

BMW had been selling military-spec R12 motorcycles to the German army since it introduced the model in 1935. The German army used sidecar-equipped motorcycles in a primary transportation role, much like the Allies used the ubiquitous Jeeps. The side-valve, single-carb R12 was easy to maintain and reliable under demanding army use. In fact, BMW continued to sell the R12 to the military until its production was finally ceased in 1942.

In 1937, the army asked both BMW and its rival, Zundapp, to build new 750-cc motorcycles to military specifications. Some of the army's specifications included:

- *Payload capacity of 500 kilograms (the equivalent of three fully armed and equipped soldiers)*
- *Capable of 80-kilometer-per-hour cruising speed when fully burdened*
- *Ability to maintain a "marching speed" of 2 kilometers per hour without overheating*

- *Minimum ground clearance of 150 millimeters, plus the ability to accommodate tire chains for snowy conditions*

Zundapp's engineers developed the robust KS750 to meet the German military's specifications. The Zundapp was powered by an air-cooled 170-degree V-twin engine that was very similar in design to the BMW boxer twins. The KS750 was built on a very strong frame, was stopped by a hydraulic braking system, and incorporated a sophisticated differential that transferred power to the sidecar's wheel to improve traction.

BMW's answer to the military's request was the R75. Powering the R75 was a new OHV engine derived from R71's side-valve design. This OHV engine, dubbed the 275/2, was fed by twin Graetzin carburetors. It produced 26 horsepower at 4,000 rpm and ample torque for the heavy sidecar applications. A low compression ratio of 5.8:1 allowed the engine to burn inferior, or even synthetic, fuels as required.

Power from this stout engine was fed through a transmission that featured four on-road speeds and three (low-range) off-road speeds. A locking rear differential transmitted power to the sidecar wheel, and there was a reverse gear to make it easier to maneuver a heavily burdened sidecar rig. Another BMW innovation in the R75 was a split in the lower frame spars, which made it much easier to remove and reinstall the engine and transmission for servicing.

The military's selection committee, the GBK, preferred the Zundapp KS750 over the BMW R75, and there were two key reasons for this. First, the R75's front suspension (consisting of telescopic front fork) was collapsing under heavy loads. Second, the BMW was expensive to manufacture. BMW was offered a choice by the military committee; it could graft the Zundapp front suspension onto its R75, or it could license production of the Zundapp motorcycle. As one might imagine, BMW's executives were not eager to begin production of a competitor's motorcycle. In the end, BMW was able to ignore the Wehrmacht's request to use a competitor's design, and the company forged ahead and continued to build its R75 with the telescopic front fork.

As the war progressed, the four-wheeled Kübelwagen built by Volkswagen (VW) became the preferred army vehicle. This inexpensive transport was comparable to the Allies' Jeep and could be manufactured much more rapidly than the BMW or Zundapp motorcycles. BMW would continue to manufacture R75 motorcycles for the military until October 1944, when Allied troops overtook the Eisenach facility.

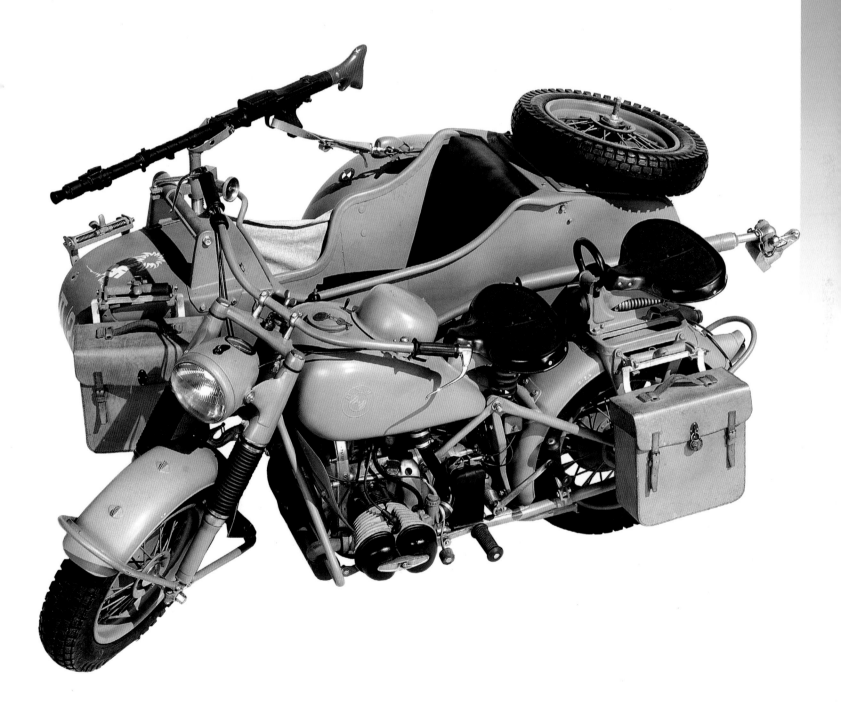

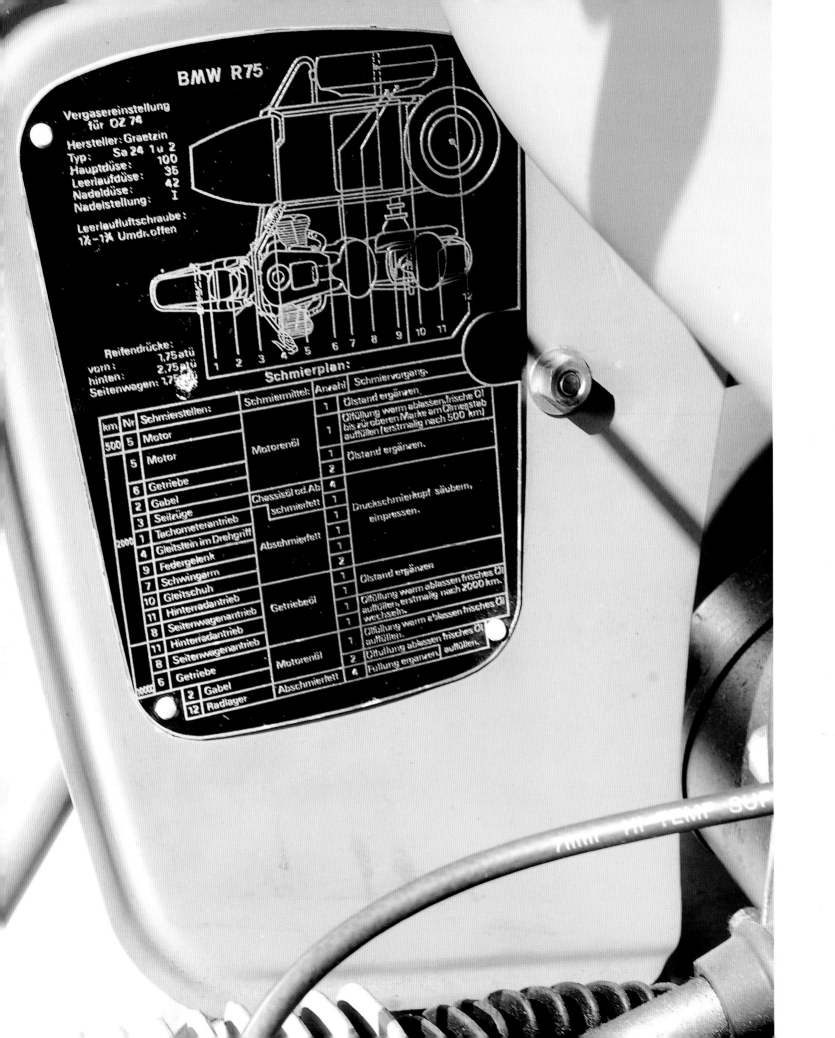

1950 R51/2 & STEIB S350

BMW resumed building motorcycles in 1949. Due to the strict rules in the immediate postwar years, BMW was forced to refrain from manufacturing vehicles without Allied approval. To make matters worse, BMW had lost much of its tooling, the factories were in shambles, and virtually all of the bike blueprints had been confiscated or destroyed by the Allied and Russian armies.

The R51 was a state-of-the-art motorcycle when it was introduced in 1938, and BMW was able to sell almost 3,800 copies before its production was halted in 1940. Positioned as an updated replacement for the excellent R5 in the 500-cc range, the prewar R51 was powered by a twin-carb OHV boxer twin that produced 24 horsepower. This engine was installed in the fully sprung 251/1 chassis with telescoping front fork and plunger-type rear suspension.

Naturally, money was tight at BMW, and the little funding that was in the coffers was earmarked for rebuilding the factories themselves. With essentially zero funds available to spend on research and development (R&D) for a new motorcycle, the engineers decided to reverse-engineer and restart manufacture of the model R51. The team tore apart several surviving R51 motorcycles and measured the dimensions of virtually every component. Using these measurements, they reconstructed the tooling and blueprints, and commenced production of the "new" R51/2 in the second half of 1949.

BMW engineers made a shrewd decision in resurrecting the R51, and, in typical fashion, they rapidly began to make a series of steady improvements to the bike. The R51/2 differed from its progenitor in a few significant areas. The engine, while based on the original's 494-cc mill, received new cylinder heads that featured coil valve springs in place of the previous hairpin valve springs. The lubrication system was improved to allow better flow to the cylinder heads. The R51/2 also received revised controls, which dispensed with the inverted pivots of the older models.

Aesthetically, the 1951 R51/3 differed little from the /2 version, but its engine was a big step forward. The R51/3 had an all-new engine, featuring a single-cam cylinder head that eliminated the long, trouble-prone cam chain of the prior model. A new engine case enclosed the magneto ignition and oil pump, yielding a very modern, clean look. There was also a new intake layout that incorporated a paper-based air filter mounted atop the transmission. Despite these improvements, however, peak output remained at 24 horsepower.

Steib sidecars were popular companions to early BMW bikes, and Steib's Zeppelin-like designs were symbolic of the styling trends of the day. Founded in 1914 as an automotive paint and upholstery shop, Steib began building sidecars in 1925 and quickly became one of the premier sidecar makers in Germany. BMW had a long relationship with Steib—BMW even commissioned Steib to build the BMW Spezial, a modified Steib TR500 sidecar that was built to BMW's specifications. By the late 1950s, automobiles had effectively killed the market for sidecar-equipped motorcycles, and Steib's sidecar sales had fallen commensurately. Sidecar production was discontinued, and Steib ultimately survived by producing a lineup of tractors and other agricultural equipment.

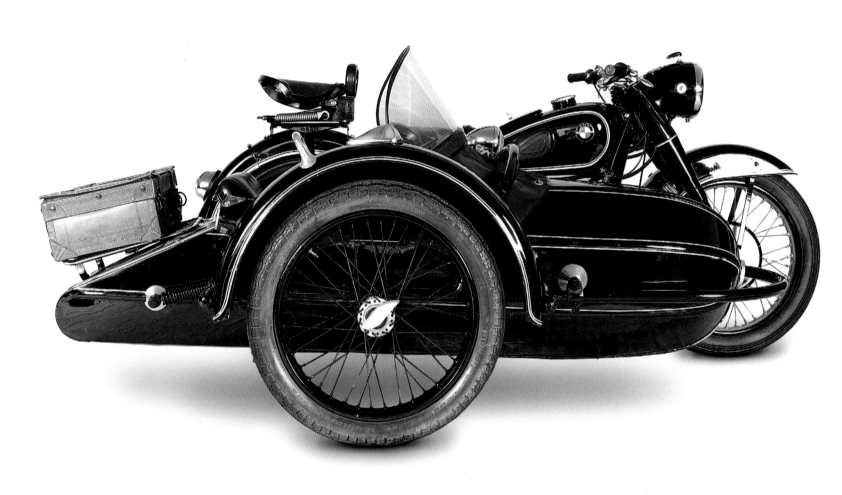

1953 R67/2

As the postwar years unfolded, BMW had to work quickly to fill out its product lineup. The German economy was in shambles, and factories (like those that BMW owned) had been major targets for Allied bombings during the war. The Allied occupation forces also restricted the vehicle manufacturing for a time after the war, and it wasn't until 1949 when BMW was allowed to resume building motorcycles. Despite huge obstacles during the late 1940s, BMW rapidly introduced (or reintroduced) models to build up its product portfolio and spark sales.

Just as is the case today, it was important to have a wide range of models to satisfy buyers with a variety of transportation needs and budgets. BMW's single-cylinder models filled out the low-priced range, powered by 250-cc air-cooled engines. In the upper ranges, BMW offered the 500-cc and 600-cc boxer twins.

The R67 appeared in 1951, positioned as a budget-minded sidecar motorcycle.

The R67 shared a chassis with the R51/3 and, later, the high-performance R68 introduced in 1952. Powered by a 594-cc OHV boxer that produced 26 horsepower, and offered at a modest price premium above the R51/3, the R67 sold 1,470 copies during 1951. While not a particularly popular model, it filled a niche in the product line.

For the next three years, R67 development mirrored that of the R51/3. An improved engine, introduced in the R67/2, enclosed the magneto and oil pump in the engine case. The R67/2 also breathed through a new intake system and had a revised valvetrain and cylinder heads. These improvements would yield a modest 2 horsepower gain, bringing the maximum output to 28 horsepower. A final version, the R67/3, arrived in 1952, bringing only minor changes like a wider rear tire.

In late 1951, BMW used the R67's chassis as the basis for a new sporting motorcycle, the R68, its top-of-the-line sportbike. The R68's 594-cc engine featured higher-compression (8.0:1) pistons, larger Bing carburetors, and a more aggressive cam profile. The result was a high-performance engine that behaved nothing like the mild-mannered lump in the R67. With 35 horsepower on tap, the R68 was propelled to speeds near 100 miles per hour—competitive with the fastest British twins. Stopping chores were handled by the 200-millimeter drums from the R51/3, including the new duplex front hub that dramatically improved front braking power. All of this performance came at a dear price, however. At almost DM 4,000, the R68 was not for everybody, and BMW sold only 1,452 copies of the bike between 1952 and 1954. The R68 is a rare and desirable bike, one of the most sought-after postwar BMW motorcycles.

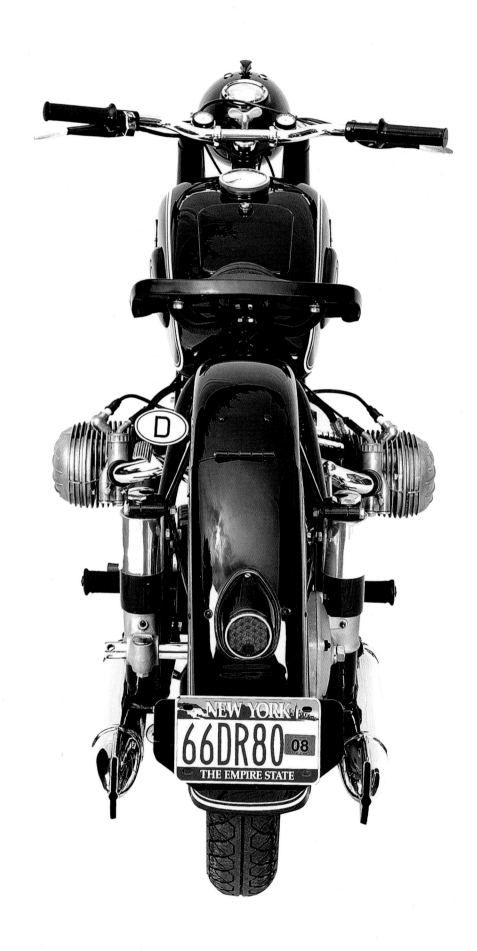

THE ART OF BMW

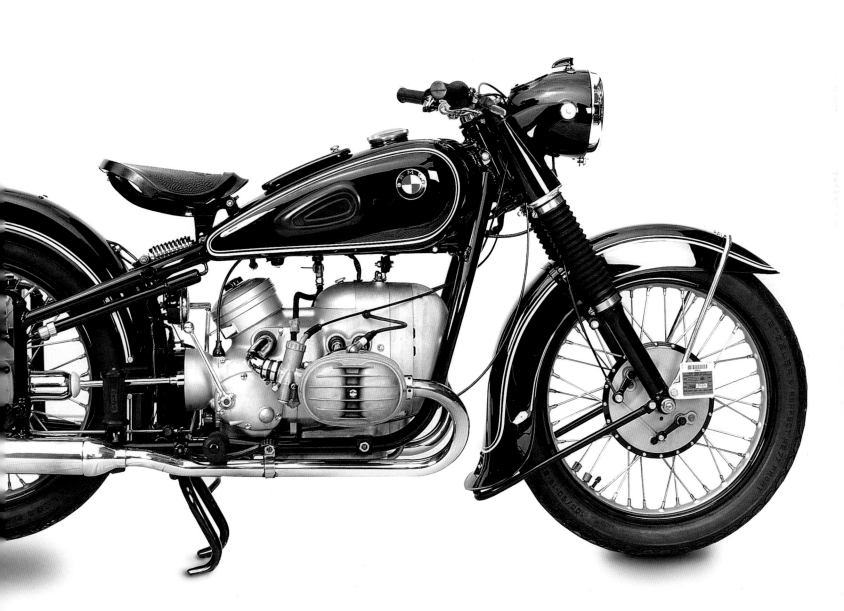

1955 R25/3

In the years immediately following World War II, Germans (and other Europeans) were clamoring for affordable transportation. Prior to the war, BMW had built considerable market share with its lineup of single-cylinder bikes. Inexpensive motorcycles were a staple of the European transportation system, and BMW's singles had established themselves as durable and well-engineered products. But the manufacture of civilian cars, trucks, and motorcycles had been curtailed during the war, and BMW hadn't built a civilian version of a motorcycle since the last batch of R71s left the factory in 1941. Shortly after the war's end in 1945, the Allied occupying forces allowed German manufacturers to resume production of motorcycles and other vehicles. However, since the rules dictated that the motorcycles displace no more than 250-cc, BMW wisely resurrected its lineup of affordable single-cylinder bikes.

BMW's first postwar single was the R24. Like the R51/2, the R24 was derived from teardowns of the prewar R23, but it incorporated some significant improvements. Its new 247-cc single-cylinder engine, dubbed the 224/1, featured an all-new cylinder head closely based on the wartime R75's. This cylinder head sported revised valve angles, new rocker arm pillars, and a two-piece valve cover. Running a modest 6.75:1 compression ratio, the engine produced 12 horsepower at 5,600 rpm and could push the R24 to a top speed of 60 miles per hour.

This engine was mounted in a familiar chassis, also called the 224/1. This tubular steel chassis featured a familiar twin-cradle design, with telescoping front fork and a rigid rear suspension. Adorning the R24 was the ubiquitous fishtail exhaust silencer, painted in a black finish due to the scarcity of chrome in postwar Germany. The 160-millimeter drums handled the braking chores at the front

and rear, providing adequate stopping power for the 268-pound bike.

The R24 was launched into a receptive marketplace; BMW received 2,500 orders for the bike in early 1948, and the factory struggled to meet the demand through that year. However, as materials shortages eased during the next two years, BMW was able to produce over 12,000 copies of this bike before it was supplanted by the R25 in 1950.

The R25 was a mildly updated version of the R24. Its engine featured a revised camshaft and a larger intake valve, but these changes did not yield significant horsepower gains. The real news about the R25 was a new frame that featured a plunger-type rear suspension, making the R25 the first BMW single to ride on a fully sprung chassis. The R25/2, appearing in 1951, was nominally different from the R25, keeping the new chassis but reverting back to the R24 engine spec. The 1953 R25/3 had some significant powertrain and chassis developments, however. A 7.0:1 compression piston, revised intake system, and larger Bing carburetor boosted output to 13 horsepower.

The singles sold very well in postwar Europe through the mid-1950s. During this period, BMW produced 23,400 R25s, 38,500 R25/2 models, and 47,700 R25/3 bikes. The success of the BMW singles brought much-needed money into the company coffers, funding the R&D and manufacture of the company's next generation of boxers and singles.

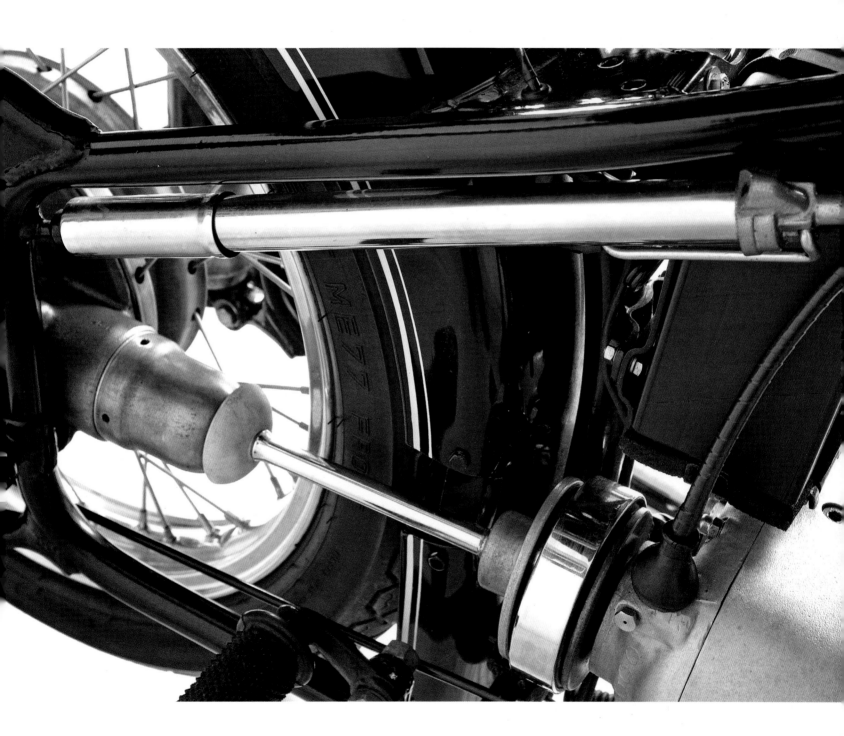

THE ART OF BMW

1965 R69S

BMW had built a fine sporting motorcycle in the R68, a bike that helped re-establish its reputation as a manufacturer of powerful and refined machinery. With its dramatic styling and excellent performance, it served as a flagship for the entire lineup and was a source of pride for the war-ravaged company. But the powerful engine was pushing the edge of the chassis's performance envelope, and BMW engineers knew they needed to make some major changes.

BMW's racing experience in the 1950s helped to test some major engine and chassis technology improvements. Foremost among these developments were new swingarm suspension geometries. For years, BMW's factory teams had successfully campaigned motorcycles that used an Earles fork front suspension. The Earles fork was a robust setup, a design that BMW licensed from Englishman Ernie Earles. The design suspended the

front axle via a swingarm and two shock absorbers that were attached to a pair of pivoting tubes descending from the steering head. The design was strong, had an innate resistance to dive under braking, and offered a well-controlled ride. An added bonus of the robust Earles fork was that it was especially well suited to sidecar duties. Racing teams had had success with this new suspension design, and it would soon prove to be a defining trait of BMW's production motorcycles as well.

The new suspension was to be offered in BMW's R50 and R69 of 1955. These bikes were based on a similar production chassis, which featured the Earles fork at the front and a standard swingarm at the rear. The new chassis retained familiar styling cues, with long loops that made them easily identifiable as BMWs, but the suspension design changes dramatically improved the bikes' ride and handling. In 1956, the Earles fork was also offered on the popular single-cylinder R26, and it

would prove to be a defining trait of BMW bikes through the next decade.

BMW first showed the R50 and R69 to the public in January 1955 and put them on sale later that year. Company sales were weak through the end of that decade, but prospects revived in 1960 when banker Herbert Quandt invested heavily in the company. Quandt's financing helped BMW launch a quartet of bikes in 1960: the R50/2, the R60/2, the R50S, and the R69S.

The R69S was considered only an updated version of the existing R69 model, but it featured a few key upgrades. Its engine displaced the same 594 cc as the R69, but the pistons now ran a higher compression ratio of 9.5:1. Stronger internals, new carbs, and a harmonic balancer on the crank helped the engine produce a respectable 42 horsepower at 7,000 rpm. A hydraulic steering damper, mounted under the lower triple clamp, tamed headshake (a noted problem exacerbated by the Earles fork's unsprung weight). While not potent enough to dethrone the racy British motorcycles of the day, the R69S would develop a following as a powerful touring bike—a forerunner to the modern Sport Tourer.

BMW offered the R69S throughout the 1960s. The motorcycle division also created an R69 version without the Earles fork, the R69US. Built exclusively for export to the United States, the R69US was mechanically identical to the R69S, but its front suspension used a telescopic fork and all of the sidecar attachment points were removed from its frame. Despite these changes, the R69 was considered a very conservative motorcycle during the 1960s, and U.S. buyers were gravitating toward domestic V-twin bikes instead.

THE ART OF BMW

1967 R60/2

1969 R60/2 Polizei

BMW introduced three new models in 1955, all using the same chassis. Dubbed the 245/1, this chassis was shared by the R50, R60, and R69 and featured a true swingarm at the rear and the Earles fork setup on the front. This suspension layout was used on racing bikes and was considered state of the art in 1955. Of course, the rear swingarm is ubiquitous on today's motorcycles, but this suspension layout was an innovation in the 1950s. BMW would wisely incorporate this design into its lineup of boxer-powered bikes.

The R50 was powered by a modestly improved 494-cc engine, previously used in the R51/3. Boasting new pistons and a slightly higher compression ratio, the R50 had 26 horsepower on tap at 5,800 rpm. Mated to a four-speed transmission that no longer had a hand-shift lever, the R50 was not a thrilling performer, but it served well as a practical sidecar motorcycle. The R50's sister bike, the

R69, was also powered by a previous-generation engine. Propulsion for the R69 came from the same 594-cc engine that was offered in the R68, a 35-horsepower boxer twin. Built with a reinforced crankshaft and mated to a new four-speed transmission, the R69 was the most sporting bike of the group. BMW targeted the new R60 directly for sidecar use. A utility-oriented replacement for the R67/3, the R60 was powered by the same torquey 26-horsepower engine. With the launch of these three bikes, BMW had nicely improved its boxer lineup, but the engineering progress didn't stop there.

The R50 and R69 were first shown to the public in January 1955, and they went on sale later that year. BMW struggled through the end of that decade, and Daimler-Benz made a takeover offer in 1959, but this offer was never accepted. Instead, BMW's fortunes were revived in 1960 by Herbert Quandt, who

invested heavily in the company. His backing allowed BMW to weather the takeover offer and the downturn in sales. Quandt's financing also made it possible for BMW to launch a quartet of bikes in 1960: the R50/2, the R60/2, the R50S, and the R69S.

Fresh capital allowed BMW to make some significant improvements to its lineup. The R50 and R60 both received updates and were rebadged the R50/2 and R60/2. The focus of the improvements centered on the engines; both bikes received stronger crankshafts and bearings, and the R60/2 got new high-compression pistons. The 7.5:1 compression ratio (up from 6.5:1) raised the R60/2's peak output to 30 horsepower at 5,800 rpm. These updates helped make the R60/2 a success, and BMW manufactured this model from 1960 to 1969.

With modest horsepower ratings and heavy chassis, the R50/2 and R60/2 were certainly not high-performance bikes. But it's important to put this in perspective. Throughout the 1950s, most of Europe (and especially Germany) was still in recovery mode after World War II. Buyers needed inexpensive, reliable transportation, and motorcycles were a very good solution. It's also no surprise that these motorcycles were widely used in commercial and police fleets. The R50/2 and R60/2 were important products for BMW, and they served their buyers very well.

THE ART OF BMW

1969–1984

As the 1960s drew to a close, BMW reevaluated its commitment to the motorcycle market. The company had increased automotive production rapidly over the course of the decade, and motorcycles were becoming much less important to its overall health. European motorcycle sales fell off dramatically during the '60s, and to make matters worse, Japanese manufacturers offered strong competition. Motorcyclists were discovering that the Japanese bikes were high-quality, technologically advanced machines, while BMW's line were based on 1950s designs with styling cues predating the war. The Beemers were not selling well in the face of this competition, and the motorcycle division's future was in jeopardy.

But BMW was not ready to give up on its motorcycles. In 1967, a photographer for a German magazine, *Das Motorrad*, snapped some spy photos of a new motorcycle running at the Nürburgring racetrack. This motorcycle was a BMW test mule and a signal to the two-wheeled world that the German manufacturer was preparing a new generation of motorcycles. Not only was BMW developing new bikes, but it was also moving motorcycle production from Munich to Berlin to afford automobile manufacture full use of the Munich plant. Bike production relocated to a former Siemens aircraft engine factory in Spandau, a Berlin suburb. BMW ceased motorcycle production at the Munich factory in May 1969, marking the end of one era and the beginning of a fresh one for Beemer bikes.

The /5 series was officially unveiled in the fall of 1969, under the watchful eye of new motorcycle operations chief, Wilfried Kramm. The bike was powered by an all-new boxer engine, and its chassis was a true clean-sheet design that addressed many of the shortcomings of the previous generations. It also represented a major style shift for BMW motorcycles.

Until this point, BMW dealers had a difficult time pitching BMWs as technologically advanced when they resembled the hardtail, side-valve bikes of the 1940s. Even if the bikes incorporated modern features, why did they look old? The /5 series challenged these preconceptions, however, and for the first time in more than 20 years, BMW had a motorcycle with a unique, modern look.

An all-new engine powered BMW's new /5 series. The engine case enclosed the crank, air filter, and starter, and the camshaft was now under the crank, moving the pushrods below the cylinders. The new design also lifted several key technical elements from BMW's automotive engines, notably an automatic tensioning cam chain and stronger crankshaft main bearings. The engine's high-pressure lubrication system didn't require the use of expensive roller bearings, and a battery and coil ignition replaced the magnetos. The cylinder heads were cast with larger valve openings, and an aggressive camshaft made this a heavy-breathing engine. Though it retained its predecessors' boxer layout, the engine was improved in almost every way. In late 1969, BMW released the R50/5, R60/5, and R75/5. Engineers employed the same stroke in all three engines, while varying cylinder bore to yield displacements of 498 cc, 599 cc, and 745 cc, respectively.

The moto world took notice of BMW's new bikes. The motorcycling press raved about the /5 series, praising its modern styling and refined manners. The bikes handled well, looked good, and were capable sporting machines. Once again BMW commanded the attention of the motorcycling world.

During the next several years, engineers and designers continued to update and improve the /5 series bikes. The early /5 bikes were known to have issues with "head shake" (front-end wobble) at high speeds. BMW engineers experimented with new forks and steering geometries,

but were not able to solve the problem quickly. In 1973, they resolved the issue by extending the swingarm and stretching the bikes' wheelbase. This change altered fore and aft weight distribution and eliminated the nervous high-speed behavior. The stretched wheelbase had some added benefits, including additional space to locate a larger battery under the seat. The new layout also allowed for relocation of the footpegs, which created more legroom behind the engine.

In 1973, BMW upgraded the bikes and gave them a new model designation: the /6 series. The slow-selling R50 disappeared from the lineup, but the R60 and R75 remained and received substantial upgrades. Now designated the R60/6 and R75/6, the bikes got new five-speed transmissions and 280-watt alternators, and the R75/5 was equipped with a much-needed front disc brake. BMW also added a new model, the R90/6, which was powered by an 898-cc version of the boxer twin. The bigger engine was simply a bored-out version of the R75 mill.

More surprises were on the way. In 1973 BMW unveiled the R90S, its most potent motorcycle yet and a true superbike. The hot R90S used a performance-tuned version of the R90/6 engine, featuring larger 38-millimeter Dell'Orto carburetors, high-compression (9.5:1) pistons, and a hotter camshaft. The bike handled very well, and its performance numbers were competitive with the excellent Japanese bikes of the day, including the Honda CB750. But what really set the R90S apart was its styling. Featuring a rounded café-racer fairing and a stellar paint job, the R90S looked unlike any other motorcycle in the world. It commanded a hefty price, too, retailing for $3,800 in the United States in 1974.

The /6 models were updated in 1977 and renamed the /7 series. Bored-out cylinders boosted the displacement of the R75 and

R90, so they became the R80/7 (798 cc) and R100/7 (980 cc). At the top of the model range was the stunning R100RS—the Hans Muth design that shocked the motorcycling world with its radical fully faired body. The R100RS defied categorization when it was introduced; it was truly the only bike of its kind ever offered to the public. Was it a sportbike? A touring bike? It was actually both, and the R100RS single-handedly created the sport-touring motorcycle category. It was later joined by the R100RT, a bike that was fully faired like the RS, but had much less sporting character. At an MSRP of $6,345 in 1979, the R100RT was the most expensive touring bike that BMW had ever offered, but the softly sprung, fully dressed tourer did not live up to its expectations, and buyers ignored the bike in droves.

The late 1970s motorcycle market was growing increasingly competitive. BMW had introduced its most technologically advanced bikes ever, yet they quickly became outdated in the face of intense competition from the land of the Rising Sun. The Japanese manufacturers were accelerating their product development efforts and were extremely active (and successful) in worldwide motorcycle racing. The Japanese bikes had sophisticated overhead-cam engines that spun to sky-high redlines. Not only were the Japanese bikes performing well, but their engineering and reliability also matched or surpassed what BMW was offering. The competition was challenging BMW motorcycle division on every front, and by the end of the '70s its future was again in doubt.

THE K-BIKES ARRIVE

At the close of the 1970s, BMW faced a major test of its commitment to making motorcycles. By 1980, BMW's U.S. sales had utterly collapsed, and the Japanese manufacturers were dominating the worldwide market. Beemers were priced far above the Japanese competition, yet they offered precious little in features or quality to justify such a comparatively high price. Rivals Triumph and Harley-Davidson faced similar endgame scenarios.

BMW had survived two world wars, so this was not a company that gave up easily. Forced either to innovate or die, BMW took the only path it knew. Borrowing engineers and designers from its automotive division, the company quietly undertook development of an entirely new range of motorcycles. At the same time, it devoted considerable resources to restoring public enthusiasm for its boxer-powered bikes.

Of course, the new model range was the inline-powered K-series. For the first time since the days of Max Friz, BMW was preparing to offer a completely new engine design. This engine was a liquid-cooled, dual overhead-cam (DOHC) four-cylinder that displaced 987 cc. The engine used Bosch electronic fuel injection and generated 90 peak horsepower. The new inline engine was mounted longitudinally in the bike's frame. Yet unlike the competition's approach, the BMW engine was turned 90 degrees from vertical, placing the cylinder head in front of the rider's left foot with the pistons traveling horizontally. This layout had several advantages over a vertical orientation—most significantly, it kept the bike's center of gravity much lower.

The first bikes to use the new engine were the K100, K100RS, and K100RT, and they were officially unveiled in the fall of 1983. The bikes shared a common powerplant and similar chassis, but were differentiated by their features. The K100 was the roadster, sporting only a small fairing to protect the rider from the wind. The RS was a sport-tourer, fully clad with fairings and including stylish hard luggage for extended road trips.

The RT was the classic touring bike, targeted to riders who wanted to put as many miles under their feet as possible.

GELÄNDSTRASSE

The K-bikes were certainly distinctive; BMW had pulled itself into the modern motorcycle design era. But the K-series bikes were not the only new products in BMW's lineup. In the early 1980s, the company created yet another new motorcycle classification: the adventure-tourer.

BMW had been formally involved in off-road racing for years, and in 1979, a BMW won the prestigious International Six Day Trials (ISDT). The bike was a purpose-built, 872-cc, boxer-twin-powered behemoth, with a special chassis featuring a monoshock rear suspension. The bike was physically huge by off-road standards, heavy, too powerful for serious off-road work, and quite unlike any other bike in BMW's stable. BMW had a production R80G/S in showrooms the following year.

The G/S (shorthand for Geländstrasse) openly defied convention. Not only was it a large dual-sport bike with a very big engine, it actually had a sophisticated chassis and an all-new rear suspension design. The Monolever rear swingarm was a single-sided, monoshock setup with an integrated driveshaft.

Nothing like it had ever been offered by a major manufacturer. Yet buyers lapped it up like a fine Bavarian Pilsner. Sure, it was too heavy for serious off-road riding, but this was mitigated by the bike's excellent on-road behavior, where it came across as light and nimble. The bike was an unqualified success, and it quickly became the best-selling bike in the BMW lineup; the GS models still continue to be extremely popular.

1974 R90S

The R90S was BMW's answer to the superbikes of the early '70s, and it was a shock to the motorcycling world.

BMW had introduced the /5 series in 1969, and the bikes had revolutionized BMW's motorcycling image. Gone were the chassis of the '50s and '60s that were reminiscent of BMW's rigid-framed early bikes. A completely new boxer engine had redefined BMW's motorcycles, and the new bikes had made BMW competitive in a market that was heavily influenced by the Japanese manufacturers. Accelerating its development schedule, in 1973 BMW brought out the /6 series: the R60/6, R75/6, and the long-anticipated sport-bike R90/6.

For about a year, there had been rumors of a 900-cc bike from BMW, and the 1973 R90/6 put those rumors to rest. Its powerplant was a bored-out version of the /6 series mill, producing 60 horse-power at 6500 rpm. Mated to a five-speed transmission, the 898-cc engine could push the R90/6 through the quarter-mile in 13.5 seconds and achieve a top speed of over 115 miles per hour.

The R90S, BMW's high-performance flagship, appeared in 1974, and it caught the entire motorcycling community by surprise. Based on the R90/6, the new bike offered even more performance with a radical styling twist. The R90S received a strengthened version of the R90/6 engine, featuring a stronger crankcase, higher compression (9.5:1) pistons, and larger 38-millimeter carburetors. The result was a boost in output to an impressive 67 horsepower. BMW's engineers gave the R90S chassis equal attention. Out front, twin vented front-disc brakes handled stopping chores, and an adjustable hydraulic steering damper mounted under the tank aided with cornering stability. The bike's long-travel suspension did a marvelous job of taming uneven pavement, offering sporty handling without compromising all-day riding comfort.

But the R90S's most striking feature wasn't its performance. With its remarkable new fairing and beautiful paint finish, the R90S set new styling standards—not just for BMW, but for the entire motorcycle industry. Created by BMW designer Hans Muth, the prominent café-racer headlight fairing was the first of its kind ever offered on a production motorcycle. The very functional fairing surrounded the round headlight and swept back toward the rider, offering wind protection and creating a perfect location for the cockpit instrumentation. On the outside, a Smoke Black finish was hand-painted on the fairing, tank, and side panels, further enhancing the bike's striking appearance.

It's difficult to overstate the R90S's impact on BMW's image. Long known for bikes that were well-built and durable, BMW made an extra leap with the R90S into the sporting motorcycle limelight. While there were certainly powerful competitors in the market, including the Honda CB750 and the 82-horsepower Kawasaki triple, none of them could match the R90S' combination of sporting capability, style, and quality. A manufacturer's suggested retail price (MSRP) of $3,800 in the United States meant that the BMW superbike was not for everyone; nevertheless, BMW's U.S. importer easily sold every copy that it was able to bring to the United States. The bike proved that buyers were willing to pay a premium for an outstanding motorcycle. The R90S's combination of power, handling, comfort, and style was unmatched in its day, and it would set the stage for more success through the 1970s.

1979 R100RS

The /6 series motorcycles were a big success, yet in typical BMW fashion, they received a steady flow of improvements. The new five-speed transmission that was introduced in the /6 series was plagued by difficult, clunky shifting. New shift forks solved this problem in the 1975 models, and this upgrade kit was offered to owners of previous years' models. The R60/6 and R75/6 models received braking system upgrades in the form of single-disc front brakes. The rotors were drilled to aid water dispersion, and the disc brakes were lighter and offered more braking power than the drums that they replaced. The R90S also received mild updates and a new Daytona Orange color option.

The R90S was a harbinger of major changes at BMW. The company had created a unique and powerful motorcycle, a true superbike that carried an image of engineering prowess and modern, powerful performance. BMW bikes were no longer regarded as conservative, sidecar-pulling motorcycles. The R90S was evidence that the company was capable of producing some of the finest sporting motorcycles in the world. Yet in the late 1970s, demand for motorcycles was declining. Slowing economies and higher oil prices caused worldwide motorcycle sales to falter in 1977, and the slide continued through 1979. In the face of these challenges, BMW was once again pushed to change and innovate or suffer significant consequences in the marketplace.

Following on the heels of the R90S's success, BMW again turned the motorcycling world on its ear with the radical R100RS. BMW designer Hans Muth created a sporting motorcycle that was unlike any other in the world. Its futuristic appearance and cutting-edge performance features would help BMW establish an entirely new motorcycle class.

The bike's most striking feature was its modern, aerodynamic bodywork.

BMW engineers used wind-tunnel testing extensively to shape the fairing's angular nose and swept windshield. The nine-piece bodywork kit included side panels that provided the rider with outstanding protection from the elements. Also integral to the bodywork design was a front spoiler that significantly reduced front-end lift and aided in stability at higher speeds. Behind the windshield, a full set of analog instruments that included an ammeter and large clock were integrated into a clean dashboard layout. A sporting saddle and low handlebars allowed the rider to "tuck in" behind the fairings, further aiding the bike's aerodynamic profile.

Motivation for the R100RS came from a punched-out version of the R90S mill. The new muscle was a direct result of a larger bore and new 94-millimeter pistons that pushed the boxer's displacement to 980 cc. The newfound power required a reinforced crankshaft, which was supported by only two main bearings and housed in the strong, compact crankcase. Atop the cylinders, the valvetrain layout was virtually identical to the R90S's, using a common camshaft to actuate pushrods that traveled beneath the cylinders. The new 980-cc engine generated 70 horsepower at 7,250 rpm and had a broad, flat torque curve. Putting this power to the ground was a five-speed transmission that was shared with all the other contemporary BMW boxers.

The R100RS excelled in its mission as BMW's (and the industry's) first modern sport-touring motorcycle. The strengthened frame and smooth-riding suspension made the bike a very satisfying mount, both in the twisties and on the long highway drones. The liter-sized boxer twin could propel the bike out of corners with authority, even when burdened with passengers and gear.

It had enough power to push the R100RS to a top speed of 125 miles per hour. The large, 6.3-gallon fuel tank allowed a very impressive fuel range of 240 miles, and the spacious hard luggage could easily accommodate the necessities for a long weekend's riding trip.

The R100RS was very desirable but expensive, with an MSRP of $4,595 in the United States. But the bike struck a perfect balance between a sporting motorcycle and a long-distance tourer, truly putting it in a class by itself. There was no shortage of buyers.

THE ART OF BMW

1983 R65LS

BMW's lineup in the late 1970s was dominated by the big boxer twins, but demand remained for smaller-displacement bikes as well. BMW responded with the R45 and R65. These small, lightweight bikes were aimed to compete against the influx of Japanese motorcycles that dominated the light- and middleweight street categories.

The R45 and R65 were introduced in 1978 to replace the outgoing R60/7. BMW had dropped its 500-cc bike from the lineup in 1974, and the R60/7 soldiered on as the smallest-displacement bike in the BMW range. It traced its roots back to 1969 and the start of /5 series production at the Spandau facility. Much had changed during the decade, and the 600-cc bikes had not been able to resist the tide of Japanese competition. BMW's answer was an all-new chassis, built shorter and smaller than its BMW siblings and designed to accommodate a new generation of smaller-displacement engines.

Inside this new R45/R65 chassis, BMW installed 474-cc and 650-cc boxer twins, respectively. The smaller-displacement R45 was intended primarily for the European market, where insurance categories favored small-displacement bikes. The R45's engine was offered in various states of tune, generating either 35 or 27 horsepower (the latter intended to qualify for reduced insurance costs). The R65's 650-cc mill produced 45 horsepower when released in 1978, rising ultimately to 50 horsepower in 1981. These small boxer engines were all mated to close-ratio five-speed transmissions.

In 1982, BMW offered the R65LS. The suffix "LS" was an abbreviation for "Luxus Sport," signifying a bit more refinement over the standard R65. The most striking feature of the R65LS was its wedge-shaped front fairing shrouding the headlight and black instrument nacelle. Designed by Hans Muth, it was more a styling feature than a true,

functional fairing. Its small size added little, if any, additional wind protection, but it lent a much more sporting appearance than the pedestrian R65 projected. The R65LS also received a revised tail-section treatment with integrated passenger grab handles. Cast-alloy wheels and black-coated exhaust furthered the performance image.

But not all changes were cosmetic. To further improve the bike's sporting character, BMW gave the R65LS some performance upgrades. Dual Brembo disc brakes up front enhanced the bike's stopping power, while a firmed up-front suspension improved handling. The R65 would never be confused with a high-speed GT bike, but the LS improvements transformed it into a respectable canyon-carving mount. The R65LS's low center of gravity and forgiving engine made it an excellent bike for the twisty roads.

The R65 and R65LS were considered BMW's entry-level bikes and priced accordingly—at least by BMW standards. The market told a different story. Throughout the 1970s, Japanese manufacturers had increased their motorcycle production capacities at a rapid rate. By the late '70s, Japanese motorcycles were exported worldwide, flooding the U.S. and European markets. These inexpensive, well-built bikes sold at value prices redefined what an entry-level motorcycle was. Against this backdrop, BMW listed its R65LS at a premium MSRP of $4,000 in the United States, $400 more than the standard R65. Many other bikes offered more horsepower and sold at lower prices, limiting BMW's sales.

THE ART OF BMW

THE ART OF BMW

1984–PRESENT

Much to the purists' surprise, the K-bikes did not bring about a funeral for the boxer-twins. For awhile in the mid-1980s, this was certainly a possibility—BMW discontinued the 980-cc boxer in 1984. But a segment of the market remained devoted to the traditional boxer layout. The G/S bikes' success only enhanced this segment's enthusiasm.

In 1986, BMW reintroduced the liter-sized boxer. This was not the same 980-cc engine that had been discontinued in 1984, however. Instead, BMW bored out the R80's smaller 797-cc boxer to the liter mark. This engine was then offered in the resurrected R100RS and RT models, which also incorporated a version of the Monolever rear suspension that had proven successful on the G/S.

Resuscitating the airhead boxer in the '80s proved to be a prescient move for BMW. The company easily could have abandoned its heritage and produced nothing but liquid-cooled fours, triples, and twins. The air-cooled boxer lineage traced back to Max Friz's R32, though, and dropping this engine family could have alienated a significant portion of BMW's traditional clientele. The better move was to breathe new life into the boxer, refining a breed that was distinctive and innovative. With its unique boxer legacy, BMW offered individuality in a market increasingly dominated by the "UJM," or "universal Japanese motorcycle."

BMW had again found its footing, and the company's motorcycle product-development efforts gained new momentum through the late '80s. Three-cylinder variants of the K-series were introduced in 1985: the 750-cc K75 bikes. The big GS bikes also featured new technology. The '87 R100GS, for example, was the first BMW to utilize the new Paralever rear suspension. One flagship motorcycle showcased all of BMW's advancements: the K1.

The K1 feasted at the technology buffet table, boasting anti-lock braking system (ABS), electronic fuel injection, four-valve heads, and Paralever suspension all wrapped in the most aerodynamic, unique bodywork that BMW had ever crafted. Intended to compete with the best of the Japanese superbikes, the K1 was BMW's shot at the title. Unfortunately, the K1 fell short of its mark. The big bike that tacked on all of the company's finest gadgetry was consequently *big*. Hampered by a very high curb weight and a gentlemen's agreement among German manufacturers to cap output at 100 horsepower, the K1 was not the bike that BMW had intended to offer. The company's rolling technology showcase reminded BMW that a good motorcycle is more than the sum of its parts.

While the K1 never met its sales objectives, the bike served as an important test bed for technologies that would find their way into the rest of the BMW lineup. ABS would ultimately be offered across all of BMW's motorcycle lines—its safety benefits were just too valuable in real-world riding. The K1 engine's four-valve head design was also significant, ultimately spreading throughout the K-series.

BMW's planners recognized an opportunity to grow the worldwide motorcycle business by reaching out to new market segments. Management had paid much attention to the large-displacement K- and R-series motorcycles, but for years BMW had not offered affordable, entry-level bikes. To remedy this situation, the company dipped its toes into unfamiliar waters and explored a collaboration with another motorcycle manufacturer.

BMW began to develop a relationship with Austria's Rotax in 1994. In that year, BMW executives visited an Aprilia factory in Italy, where Aprilia was manufacturing its new Pegaso 650. Aprilia had enlisted Rotax to produce a liquid-cooled, five-valve, single-cylinder engine for the Pegaso, and the completed Rotax engines were shipped directly to the Aprilia factory. BMW executives were impressed with the collaborative arrangement, and they welcomed the opportunity to add a single-cylinder motorcycle to the product portfolio. They immediately began to discuss a deal, and the result was the BMW F650, also called the Funduro. This new model was powered by a four-valve 650-cc Rotax engine, and the motorcycle was assembled by Aprilia at the Italian factory. BMW had completely outsourced this motorcycle, so many purists do not consider it a "true" BMW. But the F650 provided the much-needed entry-level model for BMW, and the relationship with Rotax continues to this day. This relationship led to the development of the mid-sized F800 bikes introduced in 2006.

Development work continued on the boxer engine, too. In 1993, BMW unveiled the new Oilhead—a complete redesign and modernization of the venerable boxer twin. It shared the same layout that Max Friz had used in the original R32, but the redesigned engine combined air and oil circulation to cool its Nikasil coated cylinders. A new valvetrain made four-valve heads a reality, without pushing the cylinder heads out to the point where they affected cornering clearance. The Oilhead would again revitalize the boxer engine layout and set the stage for today's evolution of the Oilhead, dubbed the Hexhead.

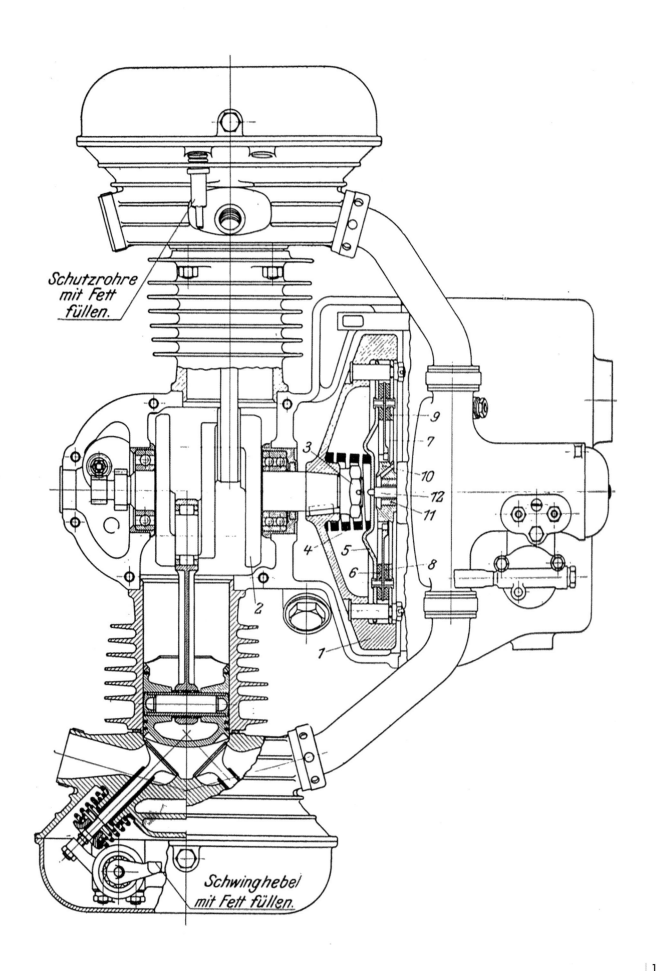

Schutzrohre
mit Fett
füllen.

Schwinghebel
mit Fett füllen.

1990 K1

In a radical departure from the air-cooled boxers, BMW built its K-bikes. Powered by the liquid-cooled three- and four-cylinder engines, the K-bikes represented new technological territory for BMW's motorcycle engineers and designers.

Japanese manufacturers had redefined supersport motorcycles in the late 1980s. With lightweight aluminum perimeter chassis, high-revving DOHC inline fours, and fully faired bodywork, Japanese superbikes like the Yamaha FZRs and Honda CBRs were setting increasingly higher performance benchmarks. These bikes were direct descendants of the race bikes of the period, and the pace of engine and chassis technology development was very rapid. The 1990 K1 was BMW's salvo into these superbike wars and was to be a tour de force of BMW's technological prowess. The company's goal was to incorporate its finest engine and chassis technology into a motorcycle that could compete against the current crop of supersports.

The K1 was based on the K100, which was introduced in 1983. Built as a styling and engineering exercise, the first scale prototype of the K1 was shown at the Time Motion exhibition in 1984. The final form was shown to BMW management in the summer of 1986, where management gave the greenlight to the production of BMW's superbike. The bike was shown to the public at the Cologne motor show in 1988.

The K1's styling is very striking and unlike that of any other BMW motorcycle built before or since. From its shrouded front wheel to its unique tail section, this BMW was designed with the pure intent to minimize wind resistance. To achieve this goal, engineers conducted extensive wind-tunnel testing to reduce the bike's drag coefficient as much as possible. The engineers were certainly successful; the K1 achieved a drag coefficient of 0.34 with the rider tucked behind the fairings. But the overall effect of

the K1's styling was polarizing, and the unique bodywork was further emphasized by the red and yellow color scheme that was standard in the bike's first production years. The bright red fairings, accented by a yellow swingarm, wheels, and body appliqués, were very unusual by BMW's conservative standards, and the coloring scheme was derogatively nicknamed "ketchup 'n' mustard."

Powering the K1 was a new four-valve version of the K-series engine. BMW had finally created a DOHC version of its inline four, which signaled that the company would continue to develop DOHC engines. Rated at an even 100 horsepower, this engine adhered to the manufacturers' "gentlemen's agreement" that forbade the sale of bikes in Germany with more than 100 horsepower.

Other technological features abounded on the K1. Bosch electronic fuel injection controlled the fuel flow and provided a host of advantages over traditional carburetors. Powerful Brembo discs handled the stopping chores, with dual discs and a single disc at the rear wheel. An antilock braking system (ABS) was optional (standard on U.S.-market bikes). The rear suspension incorporated BMW's patented Paralever suspension, marking the first use of this system on a K-series motorcycle. The Paralever integrated the shaft drive with a monoshock rear suspension and was originally introduced on the boxer-powered GS models. BMW engineers equipped the driveshaft with an extra universal joint between the engine and final drive housing, giving the shaft housing an extra pivot point. A horizontal link connected the housing and the frame, creating parallelogram suspension geometry that fed the gyrations of the driveshaft back into the frame in a back-and-forth motion, rather than an up-and-down one. Overall suspension damping was excellent, featuring a Bilstein shock at the rear wheel, and Marzocchi fork at the front.

As a flagship sporting motorcycle, the K1 was only moderately successful. A bulky drivetrain plus an abundance of accessories and features burdened the K1 with a curb weight over 600 pounds. With only 100 horsepower on tap, the smooth four-valve engine wasn't able to accelerate the K1 at a rate comparable

with the best bikes from the land of the Rising Sun. But despite the horsepower handicap, the aerodynamic bodywork enabled the bike to reach a respectable top speed of almost 150 miles per hour, and the bodywork also did a very good job of protecting the rider from the elements. However, this same bodywork inhibited inside leg movement during cornering, thus making it difficult to hustle the big K1 on the track or through twisty roads.

The K1 was in its element on high-speed open roads with sweeping turns.

BMW expected to build about 4,000 K1s per year, which it accomplished in 1989. Sales began to taper off rapidly, however, and in successive years, the bike was offered in much more subdued color schemes. Despite these efforts, a total of only 6,921 K1s were produced, and the bike is now on its way to becoming a very collectible modern BMW.

THE ART OF BMW

1995 R100GS

In an effort to improve the company's visibility in the late 1970s, BMW participated in various racing events. The racing efforts were not restricted to paved tracks, as BMW also participated in off-road events, sometimes with great success. In 1979, a factory-sponsored BMW won its class at the prestigious International Six Days Trials (ISDT) event, held that year in Poland. The rider, Fritz Witzel, won the event on an 872-cc boxer-powered prototype. BMW had developed this winning machine over the course of several years and would soon release it to the public as the new R80G/S.

Introduced in 1980, the R80G/S was unlike any other motorcycle that BMW had produced. It was a dual-sport, capable of on- and off-road use, and it was powered by BMW's 798-cc boxer twin. This engine was a retuned version of the R80/7 mill, and it produced 50 horsepower. The rear suspension was BMW's innovative Monolever, a swingarm that also housed the driveshaft and was damped by a single shock absorber. A large fuel tank offered a range of over 175 miles, and the bike handled surprisingly well on pavement.

Inadvertently, BMW had created yet another entirely new class of motorcycle: the adventure-tourer. When it was first introduced, the R80G/S was viewed as a bit of a novelty by the company and by the motorcycling community at large. Here was a bike that could easily tackle trails and fire roads, then romp down the pavement easily at supra-legal speeds. With some luggage attached, the bike was a perfect mount for trips to faraway lands (Argentina, anyone?), where road conditions varied widely and the terrain could be rugged. With its strong engine and clever features, the R80G/S was capable of conquering a trip to almost any destination.

Sales figures for the R80G/S surprised BMW. During the notoriously difficult market of the early '80s, BMW sold almost 22,000 of the bikes. After successful campaigns in the Paris-Dakar rally, 1984 brought the "Dakar" edition, featuring a larger fuel tank (8.5 gallons!), a luggage rack, and a revised seat. The R80G/S had created a buzz about BMW again, illustrating how innovative the company could be and reviving customers' interest. The R80G/S received nominal improvements until a major update in 1987. At that time, it would be rebadged the R80GS (without the "slash") and continue in production until 1996.

Joining the lineup in 1987 was the R100GS. This bike shared both its 980-cc engine and its chassis with the R100RS, though the difference between the two bikes was amazing. The 1988 R100RS was an unremarkable performer; its acceleration and handling did not even compare favorably to the R100RSs that were built in the early 1980s. But this chassis was absolutely transformed when BMW built the R100GS, due to one of BMW's finest chassis innovations—the Paralever rear suspension.

The Paralever solved one of BMW's most vexing problems: movement of the driveshaft under acceleration. As BMW's engines became more powerful, the torquing forces through the driveshaft tended to raise the rear wheel—a situation that can unsettle a bike during cornering and reduce available suspension travel when riding off-road. To solve the problem, engineers devised a double-jointed final drive layout. Inside the swingarm was a driveshaft with two universal joints. Beneath the swingarm was a strut that served as a connection point for the stay arm, and above the swingarm was a conventional single shock absorber mounted at a steep forward angle. This parallelogram layout, and the resulting suspension travel path, canceled out the effects of the driveshaft torque when accelerating. The effect on handling was dramatic, and the Paralever would eventually be adopted across the entire lineup of shaft-driven bikes.

The GS models came into being almost by accident in the early '80s, but they would prove to be pivotal products for BMW. The bikes' combination of power, technology, and adventure-touring capability found a welcoming market, and worldwide sales of the GS models would remain robust for the next 25 years.

1995 R1100RS

When the K-series was introduced in 1983, many BMW loyalists feared that the beloved boxer engines were going to be eliminated from the lineup. From an outsider's perspective, the K-series' powerful, liquid-cooled inline engines made BMW's bikes competitive with the increasingly powerful bikes from Japan. But the K-series never eliminated the boxers. Public demand for the boxer-powered bikes kept BMW's sales mix in the 1980s at about a 50/50 split between the traditional engine and the inline K-bikes. Indeed, the boxer-powered GS models were showroom stars that also received critical acclaim from the motorcycling press. Equally important was the fact that the boxer engine was nearly synonymous with BMW motorcycle heritage. In 1984, BMW began a major redesign of its boxer engine.

Over the next several years, BMW experimented with many boxer engine prototypes. Variations included valvetrain layouts, camshaft locations, and cylinder displacements. At the same time, BMW's engineers were developing a remarkable new chassis and suspension system. The new boxer engine would join the new chassis in the 1992 R1100RS.

The new boxer engine, dubbed the R259, was radically different from its predecessor. Displacing 1085 cc, the new engine was the largest-displacement boxer BMW ever offered. New cylinder heads featured a clever four-valve design, with a single, chain-driven camshaft in each cylinder head that actuated the valves via pushrods and rocker arms. Engine-management chores were handled by the sophisticated Bosch Motronic fuel injection system. New 10.7:1 pistons were 30 percent lighter than their predecessors, and they were attached to a single-piece crankshaft. The boxer's oiling system was also a very clever setup. Two separate Eaton oil pumps circulated engine oil through the cylinder heads, around the exhaust valves, through the oil cooler, and back to the engine sump. This circuit kept the operating temps in check and earned the engine the nickname "Oilhead."

For its all-new flagship sport-touring bike, BMW developed a new chassis concurrently with the new boxer engine. The engineers had specifically designed the engine to be a stressed member of the bike's chassis, supporting the front and rear subframes. To make the design even more unique, the R1100RS integrated the now-familiar Paralever rear suspension with a completely new front suspension layout called the Telelever. This suspension consisted of a large A-arm, to which the steering head and the front fork were attached. The front suspension's motions were damped by a centrally located Showa shock, and the layout provided a generous 120 millimeters of travel. Overall, the Telelever provided excellent front-wheel control at the sacrifice of a bit of front-end feel through the bars.

The new R1100RS engine and chassis were wrapped in completely new bodywork. The Telelever front suspension required a new front-fairing shape to accommodate the A-arm. This had the effect of "raising" the upper fairing and giving the R1100RS a unique silhouette. BMW's fully faired bikes spent considerable time in the wind tunnel, and the R1100RS was no exception. Its side panels swept above and below the protruding cylinder heads, and flowed back into a tapered tail section. The result was a sporting body that was aerodynamic, stylish, and provided excellent protection from the elements.

Weighing in at 526 pounds (wet), the R1100RS was not a lightweight, but the new boxer engine, producing 90 horsepower, was ideally suited to this motorcycle. The engine had plenty of power for high-speed transit, yet its excellent fuel economy endowed the bike with a range of over 300 miles on a single (6.1 gallon) tank of fuel.

Later versions of the R1100RS received incremental improvements, like an adjustable windscreen, adjustable handlebars, and a new Showa shock for the front end.

The R1100RS sold well, and it soon overtook the excellent K100RS as BMW's premier sport-touring bike. However, sales of the R1100RS were eclipsed by both the R1100RT and R1100GS bikes.

THE ART OF BMW

2007 F800S & F800ST

In the spring of 2006, BMW unveiled a completely new lineup of middleweight motorcycles. Based on a new parallel twin engine, the bikes were labeled the F800 series. This series bridged the gap between the F650 singles and the large-displacement boxers and K-bikes. This new mid-range motorcycle rolled off the assembly line of BMW's Berlin factory powered by a Rotax engine from Austria and jointly designed by BMW and BRP-Rotax. The engines were completely ready for installation when shipped to BMW's Berlin facility. During development, BMW experimented with various engine configurations including V-twins, but the parallel twin was selected by virtue of its compact dimensions and excellent power potential.

The heart of the F800 series, which includes the F800S sportbike, the F800ST sport-tourer, and the F800GS adventure-tourer, is its all-new liquid-cooled powerplant. Displacing 798 cc, the parallel twin features a four-valve cylinder head with DOHCs. The oversquare (82-millimeter) pistons have a 12:1 compression ratio, requiring premium fuel to keep detonation at bay. The pistons have a 360-degree firing sequence, meaning that they travel in tandem, with one on the "power" stroke while the other is on the "exhaust" stroke. To counter the vibrations inherent in a parallel-twin layout, BMW and Rotax engineered a unique counterbalancing system. Attached to the crank is a "dummy" connecting rod, offset 180 degrees to the pistons' rods. The effect of the third connecting rod cancels out vibrations, which produces the same effect as a separate counterbalancer, but BMW's solution doesn't penalize with the clatter that is present with conventional balance shafts. Clever.

The F800 series utilizes an all-new aluminum chassis. The design supports the engine from above and has a subframe that incorporates the seat and footpegs.

The chassis layout locates the fuel tank beneath the seat, making way for a tall air box above the engine. The front suspension is a conventional telescopic fork setup, and at the rear is BMW's single-sided Monolever swingarm, which accommodates the toothed-belt final drive and positions the rear shock at a steep angle. This rear suspension setup offers easy access to the rear wheel and gives the F800 a clean profile.

In keeping with the bike's mission, the control layout of the F800S is aggressive. The seating position and handlebars are low, positioning the rider down in the saddle and helping to keep the overall center of gravity as low as possible.

The F800ST, the sport-touring version, has some additional standard features that are not found on the F800S. A higher windscreen and more extensive lower fairings provide protection from the elements and improve aerodynamics. The raised handlebar creates a more relaxed riding position that belies the bike's mission as a touring mount. Luggage racks are standard, and F800ST buyers can purchase BMW's expandable hard luggage to carry enough gear for a long weekend's road trip. This luggage appears compact, but when fully expanded can easily accommodate a full-face helmet.

THE ART OF BMW

2007 G650X

In another radical move, BMW dramatically altered its product portfolio with the G650 series. To produce these bikes, BMW enlisted the help of Aprilia (bike design) and BRP-Rotax (engine manufacturing), and final assembly takes place at Aprilia's manufacturing facility in Noale, Italy. The series comprises three unique interpretations of a modern off-road bike: the Xcountry, the Xchallenge, and the Xmoto (the "X" is spoken as "cross"). The Xcountry has a "scrambler" style and is the most conventional dual-sport bike of the trio. The Xchallenge is characterized as a "hard enduro" bike, set up for aggressive off-road riding. Finally, the Xmoto is a supermoto-style bike, featuring a similar suspension to that on the Xchallenge, but with cast wheels shod with sportbike rubber. The G650 series is very different from BMW's traditional street lineup, and it gives the company an entry into the large worldwide market for off-road and dual-sport motorcycles.

The G650 is based on a chassis similar to the F650's. A steel main frame supports the steering head and attaches the swingarm at the rear. Smaller aluminum subframes support the seat and also connect down to the front of the engine. The G650 shares the same underseat fuel tank location as the F650, which lowers the bike's center of gravity and makes room for a tall air box above the engine. The engine itself is a fully stressed frame member, and it attaches via a reinforced point on the cylinder head. The result is a very compact, rigid chassis layout. The G650 bikes weigh in at about 60 pounds less than an F650GS.

Powering the G650 series is a 652-cc liquid-cooled single derived from the F650 models. It shares key features (like its balance shaft) with the latter, but uses lighter-weight components where possible. Featuring a DOHC four-valve head, an 11.5:1 compression ratio, and BMW's BMS-C II electronic fuel injection, the engine produces a peak of 53 horsepower at 7,000 rpm. The fuel injection system, in conjunction with a catalytic converter, helps the G650 bikes meet stringent exhaust emissions standards. An added benefit of the BMW engine-management system is its tuning flexibility. BMW is able to create custom maps for the air/fuel mixture that can tailor the engine's power curve to match the needs of the individual bikes. The engine is also efficient; its 53-mile-per-gallon fuel rating gives the bike a range of 155 miles per tankful of premium fuel.

In keeping with the bikes' missions, the suspension is heavily oriented to off-road work. The Marzocchi front fork provides 9.4 inches of travel on the Xcountry and 10.6 inches of travel on the Xmoto and Xchallenge. At the rear, a conventional gas-charged shock controls the Xcountry and Xmoto suspensions, while the Xchallenge uses an air-suspension rear shock. The air shock has an inherent progressive spring rate and does not need a conventional steel spring. The air system actually becomes more effective when heat builds up—the opposite of what happens to an oil-filled shock when it gets hot—and BMW provides a compact manual air pump with the bike to facilitate trail-side suspension adjustments.

While closely related in overall design, each of bikes has a very different character. The Xcountry is the most forgiving of the three. It's a fairly conventional dual-sport bike that has a plush suspension and good on-road handling. Shod with street-oriented dual-sport tires, it can tackle some light trail-riding and still be very road-worthy for the ride home. The Xchallenge makes no pretense about its intent—it is a hardcore enduro bike that just happens to be road legal. Its unique air suspension handles rough trails with aplomb, and the aggressive tires on stout spoke wheels are intended for serious dirty work. The last of the trio, the Xmoto, is a modern interpretation of the street-legal supermoto bike. Its Metzeler high-performance tires mounted on Marchesini alloy wheels belie its mission as a supermoto/hooligan bike. The Xmoto can achieve ridiculous lean angles.

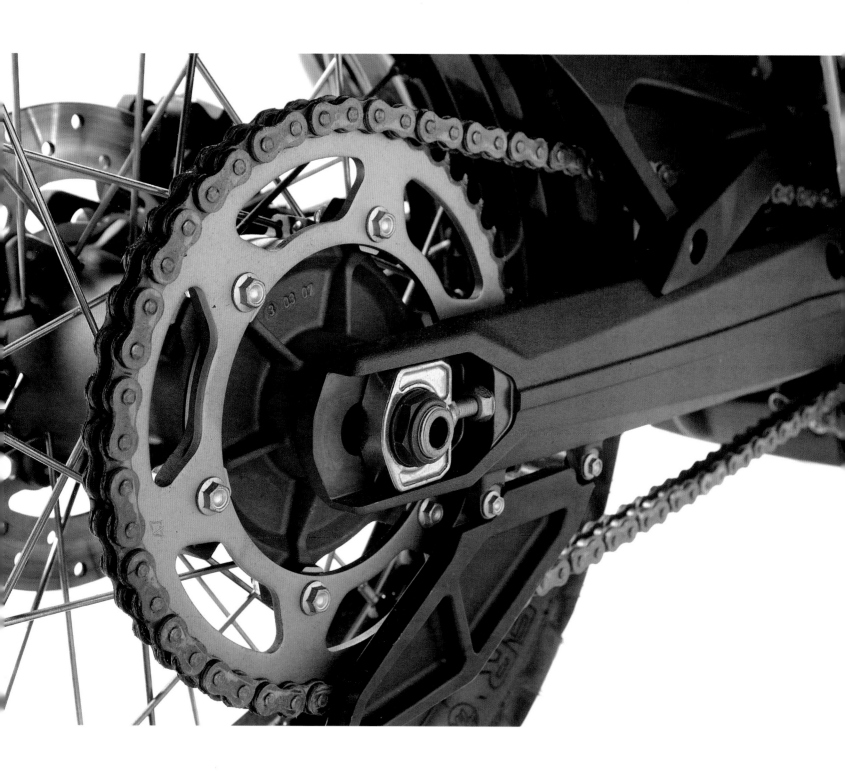

THE ART OF BMW

2007 K1200S

BMW's K-series flagship was unveiled to the motorcycling press in the fall of 2004, but the event was a major disappointment. The new bike was plagued with problems; most notable was a fuel injection system that needed major re-mapping to smooth out engine response. This launch was certainly an embarrassment for BMW, and it delayed the public launch by almost a year.

But the wait was worth it. The fuel injection was completely retuned, giving the bike excellent throttle response and making the most of the impressive output available from the 1,200-cc inline four. It also allowed the press to focus on the bike's amazing technology.

The heart of the K1200S is its powerplant; the liquid-cooled transverse four-cylinder is among the most tractable inline engines available. Displacing 1,157 cc, the DOHC four-valve engine features twin counter-rotating balance shafts that isolate vibration. BMW's electronic fuel injection is programmed for smoothness, compensating for abrupt throttle closure inputs by intervening and smoothing out the engine's actual throttle closure. The engine is rated at 167 horsepower, and it has a broad power band pulling smoothly from 2,000 rpm all the way to its 10,750-rpm redline. The six-speed transmission takes full advantage of this broad power band, and its tall gearing allows relaxed cruising in top gear. At 80 miles per hour, the engine is spinning a leisurely 4,800 rpm. This is the most potent engine BMW has ever offered, and when wound out, it can propel the K1200S to a top speed of over 170 miles per hour.

In keeping with its role as the K-series' sporting flagship, the chassis features BMW's newest suspension technology. At the rear of the bike is the familiar Paralever monoshock swingarm, while at the front is the Duolever suspension. The Duolever is nothing like a traditional telescopic front fork; instead, it uses hollow, rigid cast-aluminum tubes. The fork pivots on a pair of A-arms that behave like a double-wishbone suspension on an automobile. The arms are connected to a single shock, and the steering is stabilized with the help of an oil-filled steering damper.

The effect of the Duolever setup is profound, and the suspension behaves very differently from a conventional setup. Under cornering, the suspension compresses, yet this compression is isolated from affecting the bike's steering. Under braking, the suspension does not dive since it has an inherent anti-dive characteristic that is not affected by a shift in weight distribution. The bike can be trail-braked into a corner (much like an automobile), since the suspension will not be unsettled by mid-corner braking or steering inputs. The overall effect is difficult to describe, but the K1200S's handling capabilities are unlike any conventionally suspended motorcycle on the market.

To further enhance performance, the K1200S can be fitted with BMW's optional Electronic Suspension Adjustment (ESA) system, which allows the rider to adjust the suspension. Using a button on the left handlebar, the rider can select between three spring preload settings: solo, solo plus luggage, and two-up. Once the bike is underway, the computer calibrates the suspension damping to meet the rider's needs. The system maximizes ride quality and takes virtually all the guesswork out of suspension tuning. It also allows the rider to select between "Sport," "Normal," and "Comfort" damping modes while on the fly. Some critics believe that a rider can do a better job of calibrating a bike's suspension via manual adjustments, but it's difficult to imagine that an average rider would be able to replicate the ESA system's capabilities through its nine possible preload/damping combinations.

All of the technology is wrapped in a very stylish package. From its angular nose and creased flanks to its upswept tail section, the K1200S looks the part of a rapid transit tool. The aerodynamic bodywork does an excellent job of protecting the rider from the wind blast and shielding the rider's torso and legs, while nicely controlling the wind that flows around the rider's head and shoulders. The styling would also set a precedent for other BMW bikes to follow, including the F800ST.

BMW may have stumbled a bit at the introduction of the K1200S, but the end result is a stunning machine that set the stage for a new family of high-performance K-bikes.

THE ART OF BMW

2007 K1200R

Muscular. Edgy. Potent. Unusual. Striking. Aggressive. All of these are words that can describe the K1200R. This is a bike that revels in being different—clearly not the bike for someone who wants to blend in. The K1200R is a naked version of the K1200S. Its powertrain, chassis, suspension, and electronics are all derived directly from the fully faired S model, but as the term "naked" implies there is no bodywork to hide the mechanical bits. Everything is on display, and the K1200R is resplendent in its dramatic styling and evident technology. It can be argued that the naked K1200R is the true showpiece of BMW's performance technology.

Motivation for the K1200R is the same 1,157-cc inline four that powers the K1200S. As in the S model, this engine is mounted transversely in the chassis with its cylinders angled forward at 55 degrees. The engine is integrated nicely with a cassette-type six-speed transmission, and

its forward angle also helps to keep the bike's overall center of gravity low. The DOHC four-valve cylinder head allows the engine to breathe through steeply angled intake and exhaust valves—a technology that BMW has refined during its years of Formula One racing. The 13:1 compression ratio is very high and requires premium fuel to keep detonation under control. When necessary, however, the BMW engine-management system can retard ignition timing to accommodate lower octane fuel. Twin balance shafts keep the vibrations at bay, rotating at twice the rate of the crankshaft.

The new R's engine produces 163 horsepower, only a few ponies shy of what the K1200S has on tap. The output difference is a result of a different intake system on the K1200R that features only a single Ram-Air intake snorkel, whereas the K1200S has a pair. Nonetheless, the K1200R's engine is a brute, producing a broad torque curve that peaks at 77 lb-ft

and propels the bike forward as though shot from a cannon.

The K1200R chassis shares key features with the K1200S. Up front is the Duolever suspension, with a single damper attached to the A-arms. At the rear is the familiar Paralever, though it has been incrementally improved over the years to reduce its tendency to raise or lower the rear of the bike when the throttle is opened or closed. ESA control is an option, making it easy for the rider to configure the bike's suspension preload and damping via the handlebar controls. Also, the K1200R is available with BMW's Integral ABS, an electric power-assisted braking system. This is a linked-braking system, so when the rider squeezes the lever at the handlebar, both the front and rear brakes are actuated. The foot pedal only actuates the rear brake. These controls clamp onto big 320-millimeter discs at the front wheel and a 265-millimeter rotor at the rear, and they can bring the bike to a halt from 60 miles per hour in only 120 feet.

Technology and styling aside, the K1200R is about performance, and it has that in spades. In 2006, *Motorcycle Consumer News* tested the K1200R and recorded 0–60 times of 2.85 seconds and a quarter-mile time of 10.30 seconds at 133 miles per hour. These are stellar numbers, and they put the K1200R at the top of the naked sportbike class.

Despite its high-performance intent, the K1200R is also a very comfortable bike to ride. True to the spirit of a modern naked bike, the seating position puts the rider in a rather upright position, keeping weight off the wrists and reducing fatigue. The wide handlebars offer plenty of leverage on the steering, making the bike easier to handle in slow-speed traffic. The saddle has a broad cushion that makes all-day riding a realistic proposition, and the footpegs' locations create ample legroom for even the tallest riders. To further rider comfort, the K1200R has a standard power outlet for heated clothing, and it can be ordered with optional heated handgrips to help extend the riding season into the cold months. Optional touring luggage makes the bike an ideal companion for a weekend's romp through the twisties.

Where the K1200S is BMW's refined luxury-sport bike, the K1200R is its frat-boy twin brother. While the S model wants to carve through the mountains on the way through the vineyards, the R model is likely to be found tearing through urban confines on a mission to find the nightlife.

2007 R1200GS

The big R1200GS is the latest in the evolution of the GS series. After single-handedly creating the adventure-touring bike category more than 25 years ago, BMW has set the standard to which others aspire. The newest GS is no exception.

For those who are unfamiliar with the GS, it's difficult to understand just how capable this bike is. Can it ford a stream? Check. Carve through the esses on a mountain pass? Check. Soak up ridiculously bad urban streets? Check. Devour 500 high-speed miles before lunch? Check. It's difficult to create scenarios where the big GS doesn't excel. It is unlikely that many of the world's GS owners will use the bike for a ride through Sub-Saharan Africa, yet that image of all-condition capability is a powerful one. Some owners have even been known to do an occasional track day on the adventure bikes. There's really not much that this bike

can't do, and therein lies the appeal of the R1200GS and its off-road-oriented adventure sibling. Since the inception of the adventure-touring category with the original R80G/S in 1980, BMW has continually refined its big dual-sport bikes to accommodate almost any contingency, any road, and any terrain.

Buyers have responded in droves. From the spring of 2004 through August 2007, BMW produced 100,000 copies of the R1200GS and R1200GS Adventure, setting a BMW production record for such a short period of time. The bike's success has also required BMW to add additional work shifts at the Berlin factory to meet worldwide demand. The latest R1200GS continues to be the best-selling motorcycle in BMW's lineup.

A quick look at the GS tells you that it is a unique bike. Its duck-beak front fender, extra suspension clearance, and utilitarian styling give it a formidable presence. In person, the bike is big and

can appear a bit daunting, but it has an undeniably strong presence. Even when the tank and fenders are covered in a subtle silver color, the bike still commands attention—standing head and shoulders above most other bikes (and cars) on the road. When fitted with panniers, the bike exudes an even stronger aura of function over form.

Its engine is the largest-displacement engine available in an enduro motorcycle: the latest generation of the 1,170-cc boxer twin, generating 105 horsepower and 85 lb-ft of torque. With an overhead-cam, four-valve cylinder head, and 12:1 compression, the engine is strong yet flexible. Its BMW engine-management system has been tuned to provide a very smooth power band, pulling strongly from just above idle speed all the way through its rpm range. With a broad power band, the rider doesn't need to shift often to get a strong response—an attribute that is as important on the dirt as it is on the highway.

The GS chassis shares some common layouts with other BMW bikes. A Telelever suspension controls the front wheel, and it provides a generous 7.5 inches of travel on the standard GS. At the rear, a Paralever setup provides 7.9 inches of travel and pivots in the frame, rather than in the transmission. This layout change helps strengthen the suspension and also saves weight. Braking is handled by a pair of 12-inch rotors at the front and a 10.4-inch rotor at the rear. The partial-integral power brakes can be had with optional ABS control. Since ABS may not be advantageous in off-road situations, the system can be easily switched off. Dual-sport tires on the alloy wheels (tubeless spoke wheels are an option) handle well on pavement and still provide ample traction in the dirt.

The net result is a motorcycle that can go anywhere and do everything. Sure it's a bit heavy for serious off-roading, but there are not many off-road bikes that can cruise comfortably at 100-plus miles per hour. Add in a wealth of features like a trip computer, heated grips, and a very versatile luggage rack system, and you have a bike that can do anything its owner asks.

2012

2012 K1600GT/ GTL

Shortly after the 2009 introduction of the S1000RR, BMW followed up with another knockout bike, the K1600GT. Introduced with its sibling, the K1600GTL, the powerful touring bikes reestablished BMW's position as a premier touring bike manufacturer.

The K1600GT replaced the aging K1200LT. The LT was introduced in the late 1990s and was a direct competitor to the industry-standard Honda Gold Wing. The LT's 116-horsepower, 1172cc engine was overmatched, however, by the 780 pounds of motorcycle (plus rider and gear) it was tasked to propel. The K1200LT soldiered on through the 2000s, however, and BMW's lack of R&D in its later years fed speculation that it would soon be replaced.

The rumors proved correct when the spectacular six-cylinder K1600GT appeared. The K1600GT was a clean-sheet design that showcased the latest in BMW's engineering and design prowess. The bike is centered around its all-new inline-six engine that displaced 1649cc. This engine produces 160 horsepower and a stout 129 lb-ft of torque, providing the K1600GT with a perfect powerband for a high-speed touring motorcycle. Like the supersport S1000RR, the K1600GT offers the rider three selectable engine output modes: road, rain, and dynamic. BMW is renowned for its six-cylinder automotive engines, and the inline-six engine layout has distinct design advantages. Most significantly, an inline-six has an inherent lack of vibration, due to the design's first-order smoothness. Thus, no balance shafts are required to control vibrations (a significant weight savings). There are disadvantages, however, to an inline-six: namely, the engine width. To compensate, BMW engineers designed the new inline-six to be narrow, so the cylinder bore is small and the stroke is long. These small-bore cylinders are separated by cylinder walls of only 5mm, so the engine's overall width is kept to 22 inches—scarcely wider than a typical liquid-cooled inline-four.

The chassis retains BMW's signature suspension designs, with a Duolever front suspension and a Paralever rear suspension. The Electronic Suspension Adjustment (ESA II) system allows the rider to control the suspension settings via the handlebar-mounted control. The K1600GT also features Dynamic Traction Control and anti-lock brakes.

These sophisticated chassis and engine management systems are easily managed by the rider via a thumb-operated ring controller on the left handlebar. This controller allows the rider to tailor virtually every electronic system on the bike to his desires, including the ESA, the audio/GPS/communication system, and the engine's riding modes.

One of the most innovative safety features on the K1600GTL is its Adaptive Headlight. This high-intensity discharge (HID) headlight uses a gyro-controlled mirror to aim the headlight, constantly adjusting the xenon beam to compensate for the bike's pitch and roll angles. The result is a focused headlight that grants a rider fantastic visibility through turns on a dark road. In the real world, the system works beautifully, and it is another example of the thoughtful innovations on the K1600GT.

The K1600GT is aimed at the rider who seeks performance-oriented touring, so the rider is placed in a sport-oriented position and the suspension tuning is firm. The K1600GTL differs slightly in its mission, focusing on luxury more than sport. The GTL's suspension and seating is slightly softer, and it also comes with a standard top case and additional wind protection. These additions to the GTL (plus a larger 7.0-gallon fuel tank) add 60 pounds to the GT's 703-pound curb weight.

On the road, the K1600GT feels every bit the refined touring motorcycle that one would expect. The engine is amazingly smooth through its entire powerband, and the rider comfort is superb. At highway speeds, the cockpit is calm, and the silky six-cylinder feels as though it can consume the miles. It's the perfect bike for the long-distance rider, and it reinstated BMW at the top of the touring bike world.

2012 R1200RT

The R1200RT is the purist's BMW tourer. The latest version is powered by the 1170cc DOHC boxer twin. In 2010, BMW revised the boxer heads, incorporating the DOHC valvetrain that had been introduced in the HP2 Sport. With the revised engine, the boxer makes ample torque from just off idle and also makes excellent power even as it approaches the 8,500-rpm redline. Peak output increased to 110 horsepower, and torque maxes out at 88 lb-ft. Best of all, the new twin–spark plug DOHC cylinder heads make the torque spread wider, and the engine is now more responsive than ever.

The RT can be generously equipped with rider comforts. Heated seats and handgrips keep the rider (and passenger) toasty warm. BMW/Garmin GPS navigation keeps the rider on the right road, lest he be distracted by the scenery. A radio/CD/iPod–compatible entertainment unit is also available,

so the rider can enjoy a lovely soundtrack as the road unwinds.

Functional options are available too. Automatic Stability Control is an option, as is BMW's ESA II system. This last option allows the rider to adjust the front- and rear-spring preload and rebound damping, depending on road conditions and the bike's load status. The "sport" setting keeps the suspension firm, while "normal" and "comfort" offer a more supple ride for long stretches of highway. BMW's Telelever front suspension keeps the front end from "diving" under braking, and the RT's stout brakes have excellent braking power, offering the rider plenty of feel through the lever.

The result is a refined touring bike that loves curvy roads. The upright seating position of the RT, paired with excellent maneuverability, make it an easy ride for days on end. Simply set the cruise control, move the rider-adjustable

windscreen into an appropriate position, and point the RT down the highway. The ample saddle has plenty of room for a passenger, and the hard saddlebags will accommodate enough gear for a week. On the highway, the RT has plenty of cornering clearance for aggressive cornering, and the plush ride (adjustable via the ESA II) significantly reduces rider fatigue.

BMW also produces a law-enforcement version of the RT, and it's easy to see why—it's an attractive motorcycle for police forces. The ride is comfortable, owing to supple suspension, upright seating, and easy handling. The engine produces plenty of power for high-speed riding, yet its ample torque makes it extremely tractable around the city and at very low speeds. The RT is also surprisingly nimble for such a sizable motorcycle. The boxer twin engine keeps the bike's center of gravity low, and the bike's steering allows for a surprisingly small turning circle. As a result, the BMW excels in urban settings as a patrol bike. It is capable of carrying significant amounts of police gear and electronics, and its handling is excellent at all speeds.

This boxer-powered tourer is quintessential BMW. It fuses technology, comfort, and a dose of nostalgia into a bike that simply loves the road.

2012 G650GS

In 1994, BMW's single-cylinder dual-sport broke cover. The new F650 dramatically departed from BMW's traditional formula: its engine was from Rotax, its chassis and final assembly were from Italy's Aprilia, and it had a chain final drive! Of course, BMW has had many single-cylinder motorcycles throughout its history, but the international flavor of the F650's manufacturing was difficult for the brand-faithful to appreciate.

Nevertheless, the single-cylinder models proved a sales success from the start. BMW needed to broaden its lineup and diversify its products to appeal to riders who did not want a big boxer twin engine. Small, single-cylinder bikes are lightweight and economical, and they appeal to both entry-level riders and experienced riders who seek a smaller motorcycle. Best of all, the low price point gave the F650 extra appeal in emerging markets around the world.

In 2000, the F650 received improved styling and a new fuel-injection system to replace the dual carburetors. This bumped the engine's output to 50 horsepower and improved the bike's drivability. BMW introduced another variant in 2000, the off-road-oriented F650GS Dakar edition.

When BMW introduced its single-cylinder X models in 2007, it spelled the end for the F650GS singles. Production of the singles was halted in 2008 to free up factory space in Berlin for the new 800cc parallel-twin models. The demand for the F650GS models never disappeared, however, so BMW chose to continue the F650GS model name by putting the name on a detuned version of the 800cc twin. This move confused consumers, and the detuned twin-cylinder models were discontinued in favor of the single-cylinder bike seen here. In 2010, BMW reintroduced the single-cylinder bike and named it the G650GS. It is assembled in Italy by Aprilia, with its single-cylinder engine manufactured in China by Loncin.

This latest version of the G650GS is consistent with the original F650. Its engine is the Rotax-designed fuel-injected single, producing 50 horsepower. This engine is counterbalanced and matched to a five-speed transmission, with ratios spaced well to take advantage of the single's power curve. The G650GS Sertao replaces the former Dakar model, offering significantly longer suspension travel and better off-road performance than the standard G650GS. The name *Sertao* comes from a region of Brazil and reflects the South American location of the Dakar rally.

On the highway, the G650GS works well as a commuter and a light tourer. The bike is adroit, maneuverable, and nimble in stop-and-go traffic, but it can also attain a top speed of over 100 miles per hour. Fuel economy is excellent too, typically averaging more than 60 miles per gallon. By adding a set of panniers, the G650GS can be transformed into a light tourer. Its high seating position and thoughtful ergonomics put the rider in a comfortable position, and the excellent fuel economy gives the bike a range of more than 200 miles from its 3.7-gallon underseat fuel tank.

The F650GS is true to the GS moniker, especially in Sertao trim. It's a capable dual-sport, yet it can easily be fitted as a long-distance light tourer for extended journeys. It's a bike that every BMW loyalist can appreciate.

2012 F800GS

The success of the R1200GS made it clear there were great opportunities for BMW in the dual-sport marketplace. The big boxer–powered bikes have proven to be exceptional in many regards, and they certainly have a strong following. They are big motorcycles that can be intimidating for many riders, however, and simply too heavy to suit the desires of others. On the other hand, the G650GS may be too small or underpowered to fulfill some riders' needs.

Enter the F800GS. This middleweight dual-sport offers superior off-road prowess paired with strong on-road performance. It's the perfect bike for lightweight adventure touring and frequent blasts down the local fire roads.

The F800GS is powered by a 798cc liquid-cooled parallel-twin engine. This engine produces a maximum of 75 horsepower and is tuned to produce excellent torque at low- to mid-rpms. The engine is mated to a six-speed transmission with broad ratios to suit the variety of riding situations the bike will likely encounter.

The design of the F800GS is consistent with its contemporaries in the BMW lineup. Out front is an asymmetric headlight arrangement. The "beak" above the front wheel is similar to the style of the big R1200GS, and from a profile view, the bikes are clearly related. The F800GS's fuel tank is located under the rider's seat—a feature that keeps the bike's profile thinner and lowers its center of gravity.

Buyers of the F800GS have enormous flexibility with this motorcycle. The upright seating, compliant suspension, and amenities like ABS and heated grips make it a perfectly capable commuter bike during the week. Its ride quality is excellent on the highway, so it's a fun bike to take for an evening ride across town or through the countryside. Best of all, the F800GS is an amazing adventure-touring bike.

On the road, the F800GS excels. Its highway ride is comfortable, aided by the compliant suspension and comfortable ergonomics. BMW incorporated many features to enhance on-road riding comfort, including an informative analog/LCD display, heated handlebar grips, and an optional ABS system that can easily be switched off when riding off-road. The Brembo braking system offers excellent stopping power—a key feature for a bike likely to be burdened with heavy luggage.

Off-road, the F800GS can tackle rough terrain. Its long-travel suspension absorbs big impacts and handles rough roads with aplomb. The rear shock has over 8 inches of travel and is adjustable for preload, so the rider can accommodate a passenger or luggage. Out front, the 45mm Marzocchi forks give the front end a full 9 inches of suspension travel, though they lack adjustability.

BMW offers many accessories for the bike, including heated hand grips and a lowered seat height. In addition, the accessories aftermarket has wholeheartedly embraced the smaller GS. The bike can be extensively "farkled" with accessories like auxiliary lighting, improved seating, windscreens, and various tire options. This broad array of customization options allows riders to tailor their F800GS to be exactly the motorcycle they want it to be.

Like the big boxer–powered GS models before it, the F800GS has proven to be a sales success. BMW found many buyers who were looking for a middleweight dual-sport that could be a commuter by day and an awesome adventure-touring bike on the weekends. It's a bike with a unique blend of capabilities that is true to the core of the GS mission.

2017 R nineT Scrambler

When BMW debuted the R nineT Roadster in 2013, they started a family of bikes that share a common history and set of DNA. Over the years, the family has grown, changed, and made a name for itself in the marketplace. The R nineT Scrambler is the newest family member, and it brings a great deal of character and fun disposition to the party.

The R nineT models share a common powerplant across the entire platform, a 1170cc "Oilhead" boxer that produces 110 horsepower and abundant torque. This is a proven boxer engine; the same iteration of the boxer that, until recently, powered the big GS bikes. The torque curve is flat, the thrust is turbine-smooth, and, paired to a six-speed transmission and a dry single-plate clutch, the boxer powerplant shines with every twist of the throttle.

The family now has five models that share the R nineT badge: Scrambler, Racer, Urban G/S, Pure, and the original Roadster. The Racer is dynamic and aggressive, with elongated proportions, an aggressive sport riding position, and a gorgeous half-fairing. The Pure has a simpler throwback style, a nod to the standards that defined the motorcycle mainstream through the '70s and '80s, and it is offered at a very compelling price point. The Urban G/S has a classic style harkens back to the original Gelande/ Strasse. The Roadster is the original of the R nineT family, and it is the model that was the first to roll off the Berlin assembly line in 2013 with its nameplate riveted to the steering head, just like iconic Beemers from the past.

All of which brings us to the Scrambler. The big, aggressive tires, the raised Akrapovic exhaust, and the stout skid plate help the R nineT Scrambler capture the spirit of a fun, all-purpose motorcycle. The brushed aluminum trim and gorgeous leather seat add classic style, while the standard ABS and optional ASC add a measure of modern safety. The upright riding position and nicely padded saddle gives the rider a versatile control platform for navigating through some tight back roads and powering down long stretches of highway.

The R nineT Scrambler is certainly capable on the back roads. When the pavement ends, the Scrambler can negotiate the dirt and light off-road work. The big, torquey boxer engine has power to spare, and the riding position gives the rider a feeling of control and comfort. The ABS can be disabled and the big Metzeler tires can dig into some dirt. However, the Scrambler is truly at its best in the city, where riders can take advantage of the plush seating and upright riding position as they navigate through urban sprawl and hammer down streets that haven't been resurfaced since Ed Koch was mayor.

If all the variety within the R nineT family isn't enough, there are almost endless customization options available. For example, the large two-up saddle can be removed and a solo seat can be installed on a bolt-on shortened subframe. Wheel options, heated grips, and myriad luggage options allow the rider to make an already versatile bike unique and, frankly, even more fun.

2017 S1000XR

The BMW GS models virtually created the Adventure Touring market and have defined it for decades. Over the years, the BMW Adventure model range has broadened to include small displacement single-cylinder bikes and mid-displacement liquid cooled twins, and the top-of-the-line remains the boxer-powered R1200GS models. However, the development of the S1000RR sportbike powertrain created an opportunity. BMW now had an extremely potent inline-4 to work with, and the engineers decided to tap their inner crazy.

The result? The S1000XR, a bike that is BMW's modern interpretation of a sporttourer. The potent inline-four is at the heart of the XR, sharing the same basic components as the engine in the S1000RR and the S1000R Roadster. This engine is cradled by a stout aluminum chassis, one that is built to the same rigidity standards as the S1000RR Supersport. An available Dynamic ESA semi-active suspension allows the rider to choose from two modes, Road and Dynamic; the long suspension travel allows for excellent ride quality over uneven pavement. The Dynamic ESA sends info to the traction-control and ABS systems, creating a coherent suite of chassis management electronics. The electronics are adjustable via a user-friendly dial and switch setup located on the left handlebar. The bike sits tall with a seat height that is over 33 inches. The saddle is more "sport" than "touring," but there is ample room for a rider and a passenger. The roomy ergonomics and upright rider position evoke those of the big GS bikes, but the power and handling are definitively from the sport-touring realm.

On the open highway, the S1000XR is in its element. The 999cc engine is tuned for 160 horsepower in the XR, and it can propel the bike through the standing-start ¼ mile in 10.5 seconds. To add to the sporting character, the S1000XR utilizes BMW's Shift Assistant Pro to allow clutchless up and down shifts. This engine has a broad powerband, offering a flat torque curve and tremendous power at the top end. The electronic controls allow the rider to adjust the power output, and the rain setting dampens the throttle's response a bit and reduces the peak output when appropriate. The traction control and ABS systems provide a strong measure of confidence in all conditions, whether it be tearing up the back roads or devouring the miles rapidly while two-up touring.

The suspension is taut and will inspire confidence in even the most seasoned sportbike riders. Unlike the suspension of the GS models, the XR's priority is handling on pavement. The S1000XR uses a conventional fork, rather than a Telelever, to enhance road and control feel and provide excellent feedback. The Brembo brakes provide fade-free stopping power and let the rider push into every corner just a little harder.

The S1000XR is a tremendously capable, multi-purpose road bike. If you seek to travel beyond the gravel roads, you should be shopping for a GS.

2017 C650 Sport

BMW has been active in the scooter marketplace since the early 2000s, when the company introduced the C1. The innovative C1 was BMW's first attempt to develop a unique product for the urban mobility marketplace. The C1 had a unique approach to rider safety, featuring a hard roof overhead and an automotive-style seat with a 4-point safety harness. BMW even incorporated crash testing into the development of the C1, and the scooter earned crash safety scores that were similar to compact cars from the era. Regardless, the C1 never sold in large volumes, yet the company clearly recognized the market demand for urban transportation solutions.

Fast forward to 2010, when BMW's Design Chief David Robb introduced a concept for a new generation of scooters. The Concept C Scooter debuted, a prototype for BMW's interpretation of the "maxi scooter." These are not the small, upright layouts that one typically associates with the urban scooter. Rather, they are bigger bikes with large-diameter wheels and a saddle that is comfortable for all-day riding. Potent engines mated to CVTs make the bikes useful in urban settings and provide plenty of power for riding on the open roads.

Most scooters are utilitarian, built for commuting to work and errand-running around town. The C650 Sport can certainly handle those tasks, but it is also capable of much more. BMW instilled a great deal of sporting character into the C650, starting with the powerplant. The C650 is powered by a DOHC 647cc parallel-twin with electronic fuel injection, producing 60 horsepower at 7500 rpm and 46 lb-ft of torque. In combination with the CVT, the C650 Sport can accelerate hard and achieve a top speed of over 110 miles per hour.

The C650's chassis is stout, built of tube steel with cast aluminum sections that add rigidity and save weight. Beneath the saddle, there is a large storage compartment that can hold a full-face helmet, and this space can be cleverly expanded when the bike is parked. Underneath, the suspension and braking systems are tailored to the high performance of the scooter's capabilities. The front suspension is comprised of stout 40mm USD forks, and there is 4.5 inches of travel at front and rear. The 15-inch cast aluminum wheels run 120/70 tires in front and 160/60 on the rear. In keeping with the sporting intentions, there are large 270mm disc brakes, a pair in front and a single disc on the rear with ABS control on the twin piston calipers.

On the road, the C650 Sport displays the duality of its practical and sporting character. It's perfectly at home in the daily urban grind, effortlessly gliding through traffic while the rider sits comfortably behind the protective front fairings. To aid in urban safety, BMW offers an optional Side View Assist system that uses blind spot sensors to alert a rider of other vehicles alongside. There's no clutch, no fuss, and the supple suspension absorbs the harshest of city pavement with aplomb. Once free of the tight city traffic, however, the C650 offers the rider a great deal of fun. The engine revs easily, and the C650 will accelerate rapidly to freeway speeds. The suspension provides excellent wheel control and cornering stability, and the powerful stoppers can haul the 549-pound scooter down from speed with reassuring ease.

All told, the C650 Sport offers its owner the best of both worlds. It's an urban commuting tool during the weekdays, and a sporting mount for the weekends. A practical companion and a fun playmate, engineered and built with the quality and features for which BMW is renowned.

2017 HP4

The S1000RR set a new standard for BMW performance. It was a technological tour de force, showcasing all the amazing engineering talent and design ability that BMW had to offer. But, there's always room for improvement . . . Enter the HP4, a bike that takes BMW to a new plane in performance motorcycle design and engineering. The HP4 concept debuted in 2016 at the EICMA show in Italy, the highest-profile venue in the motorcycle industry. BMW wanted to make a statement at the EICMA show, and the HP4 was the exclamation point. The HP4 is, virtually, World Superbike-level hardware that is being sold to 750 very fortunate buyers worldwide.

The most notable feature of this bike is its weight, or lack thereof. The HP4's key chassis components are made of carbon fiber, including the main frame. The one-piece main frame weighs a scant 17.2 pounds, a weight reduction of almost 9 pounds compared to the aluminum frame of the S1000RR. Unlike most carbon fiber pieces, production of this main frame is automated at the factory, where the frame has all the key pivots and races molded, rather than drilled into it. Three different carbon fiber subframes are available as options, allowing the owner a choice of seat heights. Other tasty carbon components include the wheels, which are molded in one piece and provide a 30 percent weight saving over comparable aluminum wheels. Combined with myriad other race-ready bits, the HP4 tips the scales at a featherweight 377 pounds wet.

Of course, this Superbike-quality chassis deserves an appropriate engine, and the HP4 has one. The 999cc inline-four is a hand-built factory race engine with lightened internals and forged-steel connecting rods. New camshafts and revised intake give the engine the breathing ability it needs to produce 215 horsepower and rev to its 14,500 rpm redline.

Of note, BMW has indicated that the HP4 engine is built to last for a duration of 5000 kilometers (3,106 miles) before it requires a complete factory-built and certified replacement engine. Owners should budget accordingly.

This is a racing motorcycle designed for race conditions, and it demands to be treated as such. The traction control, engine-braking, and wheelie-control settings allow the rider to tailor the engine's power output and throttle response to track conditions, and the settings can be adjusted on the fly through a wide range of intervention levels. The HP4's engine does not have the luxury of auxiliary electric cooling fans, so idling cannot be tolerated for long periods. The Superbike-spec Ohlins FGR 300 fork and Brembo GP4 PR Monoblock calipers are pure racing pieces, and they are ideally suited to the mission of the HP4. The swingarm pivot, steering head, rearsets, ride height, and gearing can all be adjusted to suit the rider's needs for a particular track. If you plan to ride the HP4 at the racetrack, be sure to bring a team mechanic along to help analyze the data from the dash computer, which monitors all of the HP4's vital functions and has the expandable capability to monitor data such as brake pressure and suspension travel.

The HP4 became available for purchase in 2017, and BMW limited production to 750 copies. Potential owners are required to sign a waiver that indicates how the bike is to be used—hopefully, they indicate that these special machines will be enjoyed often (on a racetrack only, of course). The HP4 is a showcase of BMW engineering prowess and a harbinger of what may lie ahead for BMW's highest level of performance motorcycles.

THE ART OF BMW

2017 G310R

In efforts to expand both its lineup and global presence, BMW is returning a focus to small-displacement motorcycles. BMW Motorrad has recently structured strategic partnerships with other global OEMs, and in 2013, BMW entered into an agreement with TVS of India. BMW is working feverishly to expand its sales network in India and other parts of the world where big-displacement bikes are prohibitively expensive. Their goal is to design and build small displacement motorcycles for global markets. BMW would design and engineer the BMW-badged bikes, and TVS (the third-largest motorcycle manufacturer in India) would handle the production with BMW's supervision. The first product from this new partnership is the BMW G310R. The bike was announced at the Milan Show in 2015,

and it began production a year later at the TVS Hosur plant in Tamil Nadu.

The G310R is a modern entry-level bike for BMW, offered at a competitive price of $4,750 and built to attract new riders with a naked bike styling that emulates the S1000R. The bike's power comes from a liquid-cooled DOHC single that is tilted rearward and mated to a six-speed transmission. This is a unique orientation for a modern engine, whereby the intake is located on the front of the engine and the exhaust exits at the rear. A key benefit of this layout is that it allows the engine to be located further forward in the frame. In combination with an optimized length of its aluminum swingarm, the result is a nearly perfect 50/50 weight distribution. The 313cc single produces a modest peak of 34 horsepower at 9,500 rpm and it redlines at 10,600 rpm, but it provides ample

power for an entry-level bike that weighs only 349 pounds.

The stout steel chassis and aluminum swingarm support KYB fork components that give the bike its nimble handling feel—a capable rider on the G310R will definitely have fun hustling the bike through the canyons. Braking chores are handled by a single 300mm disc on the front and a 240mm disc at the rear. ABS has been standard equipment on every Beemer since 2013, and the standard two-channel ABS braking system on the G310R benefits entry-level and experienced riders alike.

A low seat and comfortable ergonomics allow riders of all sizes to quickly acclimate to the featherweight bike. On the road, the G310R feels light and easy to handle, and excels on city streets and back roads. Around town, the single-cylinder engine has ample power for almost any situation, and its excellent fuel economy allows for a 200-mile range. On the freeway, the G310R has enough power to keep up with fast traffic, but its top speed is a modest 90 miles per hour.

The powertrain of the G310R will be the basis for a growing family of small-displacement BMW bikes. The G310GS has already debuted, and this "mini-ADV" bike is built on a mildly revised frame with GS family styling and features. More small-displacement models are promised and BMW expects a substantial aftermarket presence to develop around the small bikes.

INDEX

THE ART OF BMW